WESTMORELAND COUNTY, VIRGINIA DEEDS & WILLS

1754-1756

DEED & WILL BOOK 12 [Part 3]

And

1756-1761

DEED & WILL BOOK 13

Abstracted and published by

Mike Marshall

Westmoreland County, Virginia Deeds & Wills:
DB12, 1754-1756 and DB13, 1756-1761

Westmoreland County, Virginia
Deeds & Wills:
DB12, 1754-1756 and DB13,
1756-1761

ISBN 9798388501790

Copyright (c) March 2023 by Mike
Marshall
All rights reserved
Printed in the United States of America

Westmoreland County, Virginia Deeds & Wills:
DB12, 1754-1756 and DB13, 1756-1761

INTRODUCTION

Deed and will books can contain land transactions, mortgages, leases, bills of sale, powers of attorney, marriage contracts, estate settlements, and much more information of genealogical interest. They are a must for researching your family history.

This volume contains the remaining entries from Westmoreland County Deed and Will Book No.12, 1754-1756 [Part 3] beginning on page 320 and ending on page 337 for Courts held March 30, 1756 through May 5, 1756. The previous portions of Deed Book 12 (Pages 1-319) were published by "The Antient Press".

This volume also contains all entries from Westmoreland County Deed and Will Book No.13, 1756-1761 beginning on page 1 and ending on page 327 for Courts held through May 5, 1756 through March 21, 1761;

An every-name index adds to the value of this work.

The format of these abstracts generally follows the earlier "The Antient Press" Will and Land records published by Ruth & Sam Sparacio, and now by Heritage Books, Inc., 5810 Ruatan St., Berwyn Heights, Maryland 20740.

Notes with parenthesis "[ ]" contain additional information or clarification.

Spelling of names and places were cross checked against the following publications for accuracy.

- Colonial Lands and Roads of Westmoreland County, Virginia; [Edward J. White] 2020
- Lands and Lesser Gentry of Eastern Westmoreland County, Virginia 1650-1840s, [Edward J. White] 2014),
- Historical Atlas of Westmoreland County, Virginia; [David Wolfe Eaton] 1942
- 1755-1758 Westmoreland Count, Virginia Orders [Pamela S. Pearson] 2009
- 1758-1761 Westmoreland Count, Virginia Orders [Pamela S. Pearson] 2008

Definitions:

Ad Quod Damnum - a writ issued in proceedings (as of condemnation) to assess damages for land seized for public use

Writ of Detinue - Detinue is a writ which lies where any man comes to goods by delivery or finding and refuses to deliver them

Westmoreland County Deed and Will Book No.12, 1754-1756 [Part 3] beginning on page 320 and ending on page 337 for Courts held March 30, 1756 through May 5, 1756

Page 320.
Gray to Gray Deed
This indenture made October 3, 1755 between Nathaniel Gray and George Gray in the County of Stafford of the one part and Francis Gray in the County of Westmoreland of the other part. Witnesseth that Nathaniel Gray and George Gray in consideration of 96 pounds current money of Virginia as also for moving have sold unto Francis Gray a tract of land now in possession of James Blair at a stump near the head of a branch then along Blair's line unto a white oak standing near a

Westmoreland County, Virginia Deeds & Wills DB12, 1754-1756

spring formerly called Gammer Masseys Spring on Washington's then along Washington's line to the line of Richard Bernard thence along his line, thence up the said branch the meanders thereof to the Round Hill Church, thence along the road the several meanders thereof to the beginning together with all and singular orchards, gardens and houses edifices buildings woods underwoods timber and timber trees with all other profits and commodities thereunto belonging.
In witness whereof the parties above mentioned have hereunto set their hands and seals the day and year first mentioned.
Signed Sealed
In the presence of us: Nathan Gray
William Degge   George Gray
Gabriel Johnston
John Degge
John Strother
Sarah Strother (her mark)
Easter Martin (her mark)
Received this October 3rd, 1755 the consideration sum within mentioned paid by me the said Francis Gray
Signed Sealed & Delivered
In the presence of us: Nathan Gray
William Degge   George Gray
Gabriel Johnston
John Degge
John Strother
Sarah Strother (her mark)
Easter Martin (her mark)
Received this October 3rd, 1755 the consideration sum within mentioned paid by me the said Francis Gray
Westmoreland Sct; At a court held March 20, 1756, this deed with the receipt for consideration thereon endorsed passed from Nathaniel Gray and George Gray to Francis Gray and proved by the oaths of William Degge, Gabriel Johnston and John Degge and ordered to be recorded
Test, Recorded April 8, 1756   George Lee CCW

Page 322.
Bayne to Higdon Deed
This indenture made December 5, 1755 between Matthew Bayne and Eleanor Bayne his wife of Washington Parish in the County of Westmoreland, Planter of the one part and John Higdon of the same Parish and County of the other part. Witnesseth that Matthew Bayne and Elenor his wife in consideration of a certain bond passed by him the said Matthew Bayne to John Higdon bearing date the 14th day of March 1753 and also in consideration of the sum of 20 pounds current money whereof the said Matthew Bayne and Elinor hereby acknowledge has sold unto John Higdon the remainder of that messuage tract or tenant of land with the appurtenances lying situated and being in the Parish of Washington and County of Westmoreland containing 93 acres it being a parcel of land given to the said John Higdon by the last will and testament of James Mason, deceased and conveyed by him the said John Higdon to Matthew Bayne only accepting to himself 1 acre of the said land for a mill on the run by the said Higdon's house relation to the surveyor's plot will make appear. In witness whereof the said parties to these presents interchangeably set their hands and seals the day and year above written
Sealed and delivered in presence of
Thomas Muse   Matthew Bayne
Humphrey Pope   Elenor Bayne
Walter Anderson
Memorandum, on the fifth day of December 1755 peaceful and quiet possession was given and delivered by the within named Matthew Bayne and Elinor to John Higdon to the land mentioned together with the delivery of turf and twigg the said land to have and to hold according to the tenor of the true form and effect of the within written deed.

In presence of
Thomas Muse				Matthew Bayne
Humphrey Pope				Elenor Bayne
Walter Anderson
Westmoreland Sct. At a court held for the said County the 30th day of March 1756 Matthew Bayne came into Court and personally acknowledged this deed and delivery of seizen thereon endorsed by him passed to John Higdon to be his proper act.
Recorded the eighth day of April 1756   George Lee, CCW

Page 325.
Harrison to Middleton Bond
Know all men by these presents that I Samuel Harrison of the Parish of Cople in the County of Westmoreland and held and do stand firmly bound and indebted unto Benedict Middleton of the same Parish in County in the full and just sum of 50 pounds current money of Virginia to be paid unto the said Benedict Middleton his heirs executors administrators or assigns to which payment will and truly be made I bind myself by heirs in the whole and for the whole firmly by these presents seal with my seal and dated this 10th day of April 1756.
The condition of the above obligation is such that whereas there is a matter of controversy and dispute between the said Benedict Middleton and the said Samuel Harrison relation to the bounds of the land the said Harrison bought of James Lane and the land the said Middleton bought of John Armistead. And where the parties have mutually elected and chosen Capt. John Newton and Mr. Daniel Tebbs to settle and determine the said dispute, now if the said Samuel Harrison his heirs and assigns shall and do stand to and abide by the determination of the said John Newton and Daniel Tebbs then the above obligation to be void and of no effect, or else to remain effectual in the law.
Signed, Sealed and Delivered		Samuel Harrison
in the presence of us
Joseph Lane
Benjamin Middleton
William Hartley
Know now ye that we the said John Newton and Daniel Tebbs having heard the allegations of both parties do here upon make input in writing this award, determination and judgment between the said parties and form following; that the line made run and agreed on by and between John Armistead and James Lane hereafter confirmed and established the dividing line between the said Middleton and the said Harrison's lands, beginning at a large red oak thence extending across the said land as strait course to and by a sapling and to be marked by James Lane. and witness whereof we have hereunto set our hands and seals this 26th day of April Anno Domini 1756
Westmoreland Sct; at a Court held for the said County the 27th day of April 1756 this arbitration bond and the award thereupon between Samuel Harrison and Benedict Middleton was presented into Court by the said Middleton and on his motion was admitted to record.
Test
Recorded the 30th day of May 1756   George Lee CCW

Page 327.
Chambers to Bushrod Deed
This indenture made this sixth day of September 1754 between William Chambers of the Parish of Washington County of Westmoreland of the one part and John Bushrod of the Parish of Cople and County aforesaid of the other part. Witnesseth that William Chambers in consideration of 35 pounds current money has sold unto John Bushrod all that tract plantation or parcel of land whereon he now lives containing 60 acres being in the Parish of Washington which said land and premises being the one moiety of 120 acres purchased of John Spencer by his grandfather William Chambers and joins to the land of the heirs of the late Capt. Daniel McCarty and the said Bushrod. In witness whereof to these presents I have hereunto set my hand and affixed my seal the day and year within written.

Westmoreland County, Virginia Deeds & Wills DB12, 1754-1756

Signed sealed and delivered in presence of us   William Chambers (his mark)
Hannah McAuley, Charles Morris
Vincent Sandy (his mark), John Ariss

Page 329.
Chambers to Bushrod Bond
Know all men by these presents that I William Chambers of the Parish of Washington in County of Westmoreland am held and firmly bound and indebted unto John Bushrod of the Parish of Cople and the County aforesaid in the full and just sum of 100 pounds current money in which payment will well and truly be made, I bind myself and my heirs firmly by these presents, sealed with my seal and dated this sixth day of September 1755.
The condition of the above obligation is such whereas I William Chambers hath bargained and sold unto John Bushrod his heirs of one certain parcel or tract of land containing 60 acres and being in the Parish of Westmoreland and County aforesaid whereon he now lives and by a certain deed of indenture of bargain and sale having even day with these presents relation thereunto may more fully appear.
Now if the aforesaid William Chambers his heirs and assigns shall from time to time and of all times forever hereafter observed perform fulfill keep all and singular the articles covenants promises and agreements in the said indenture contain comprised mentioned on his part ought to be observed perform fulfill and in all respects duly truly and faithfully complied thereunto in the above obligation to be void and of non-effect otherwise to stand remain and be in full force power and effect.
Signed sealed and delivered in presence of us   William Chambers (his mark)
Hannah McAuley
Charles Morris
Vincent Sandy (his mark)
John Ariss
Westmoreland Sct; at a Court held for the said County the 30th day of March 1756 this deed and bond for performance of covenants passed from William Chambers to John Bushrod him passed by the oaths of John Harris and Vincent Sandy two of the witnesses thereto and ordered to be lodged for further proof.
Test,
George Lee CCW.
Westmoreland Sct; at a Court held for the said County the 27th day of April 1756 this deed and bond more fully proved by the oath of Charles Morris another witness thereto and thereupon ordered to be recorded.
Recorded the 4th day of May 1756   George Lee CCW

Page 330.
Higdon to Butler Deed
Indenture made 27th day of April 1756 between John Higdon of the Parish of Washington and County of Westmoreland, planter of the one part and Laurence Butler of the Parish and County aforesaid, Gent., of the other part. Witnesseth that John Higdon in consideration of the sum of 20 pounds current money paid by Laurence Butler has sold a certain parcel of land situate lying and being in the Parish aforesaid on Mattox Creek containing 30 acres or thereabouts and bounded as follows; Beginning at a small red oak standing on the west side of a small branch dividing this land from the land of the said Laurence Butler thence up the said branch South 35° West 20 poles thence South 22° West 16 poles to another small branch thence South 46° West up the last mentioned branch 10 poles West to a marked beech, thence South 40° West along a line of marked trees 92 poles to the easternmost bounds of a white marsh, thence North 64° West 35 poles to a marked maple, thence North 18 poles East 28 poles to a gum standing near the head of the said Higdon's spring branch thence North 35° East 46 poles 12 links to a white oak thence North 70° East to the beginning. Which said parcel of land bounded and described as aforesaid is a part of a larger tract of land given and devised to John Higdon in fee tail by the last will and testament of James Mason, and the said John Higdon being seized as tenant in fee tail and minded and willing to sell and dispose of the same did pursuant to the act of assembly in such cases made

and provided sue out of the secretary's office of this colony his majesties writ for the nature of land ad quod dammum to the sheriff of said County of Westmoreland directed upon the execution of which said writ the jury impaneled thereon upon their oaths having returned that the said lands are of less value than £200 and that they are not contiguous or adjoining to the other entail lands in the possession of the said John; the said John Higdon thereupon did sell and convey the said lands and premises to one Matthew Bayne of the County of Westmoreland in fee simple as by the said writ inquisition and conveyance remaining on recorded in the general Court of this colony may more freely and at large appear and the said Matthew Bayne for a valuable consideration to him in hand paid did bargain sell and make over to the said John Higdon in fee simple part of the said tract of land of which the above recited premises hereby sold and conveyed or intended to be hereby sold and conveyed or parcel as by the said indenture of record in the County Court of Westmoreland may more fully and at large appear.

In Witness whereof the said John Higdon hath hereunto set his hand and seal the day and year above written.

Signed Sealed and delivered in presence of   John Higdon

Received of the within named Law Butler 20 pounds being the consideration money expressed to be paid to me upon perfection hereof. As Witness my hand this twenty seventh day of April 1756
       John Higdon

Westmoreland Sct. At a court held for the said county the 27th day of April 1756 John Higdon came into court and personally acknowledged this deed and the receipt for consideration thereon endorsed by him passed to Laurence Butler, to be his proper act which on motion of the said Butler was ordered to be recorded.

Recorded the 4th day of April 1756   George Lee CCW

Page 332.
Ashton to Storke Deed

This Indenture made the twenty sixth day of April 1756 between Henry Ashton of the Parish of Washington and the County of Westmoreland of the one part and John Storke of the Parish and county aforesaid of the other part. Witnesseth that Henry Ashton in consideration of 322 pounds 10 shillings current money of Virginia paid by John Storke has sold a tract or parcel o land situate lying and being upon Nominy Creek in the Parish of Cople and Westmoreland County containing 300 acres more or less and bounded easterly and southerly upon Nominy Creek, westerly upon the land formerly belonging to Richard Hawkins, Northerly upon a small creek called Kings Creek which divides the land from a tract formerly granted to Col. Thomas Speke which said tract of land was sold and conveyed by Mr. John Sturman to Col. Henry Ashton by indenture having date the fifth of October 1712, and by Henry Ashton in his last will and testament bearing date the twenty sixth day of February, 1730 given and devised in fee simple to his son John Ashton, who dying an infant under the age of 21 years without issue the said tract descended to the said Henry Ashton as heir at law to the said John. In witness whereof the said Henry Ashton together with Jane Ashton his wife have hereunto set their hands and seals the day and year first above written.

Signed Sealed and delivered in presence of   Henry Ashton
William Bernard   Jane Ashton
John Mason
Thomas Butler

Westmoreland Sct. At a court held for the said county the 27th date of April 1756
This deed and receipt for consideration thereon endorsed and passed by the oaths of William Bernard, John Mason and Thomas Butler, witnesses thereto and thereupon ordered to be recorded
Test
Recorded the 4th day of May 1756   George Lee CCW

Page 335.
Settle to Martin Deed

This indenture made the 11th day of November 1755 between Francis Settle of Westmoreland and Sarah Settle his wife of the one part and John Martin, Gent., of the county aforesaid of the other part. Witnesseth that Francis Settle in consideration of 50 pounds current money of Virginia paid by

Westmoreland County, Virginia Deeds & Wills DB12, 1754-1756

John Martin has sold two tracts or parcels messuages or tenements of land containing by estimation 600 acres lying and being on the head of Weedon's Dam in Westmoreland County, and by him purchased from John Triplett & the executors of George Blackmore, deceased.

In witness whereof the said parties to these presents have hereunto interchangeably set their hands and seals the day and year first above written.

Sealed and delivered in the presents of us   Francis Settle
Test   Sarah Settle (her mark)
John Mason
Thomas Butler
John Degge
John Hurley

Westmoreland Sct. At a court held for the said county the 30th date of March 1756
This deed passed from Francis Settle and Sarah his wife to John Martin, Gent., was proved by the oaths of Thomas Butler and John Degge, two of the witnesses thereto and thereupon ordered to be recorded
Test   George Lee CCW

Westmoreland Sct. At a court held for the said county the 27th date of April 1756
This deed was fully proved by the oath of John Mason another witness thereto and thereupon ordered to be recorded
Test
Recorded the 5th day of May 1756   George Lee CCW

End of Westmoreland County, Virginia Deed & Book 12

Westmoreland County Deed and Will Book No.13, 1756-1761 beginning on page 1 and ending on page 327 for Courts held through May 5, 1756 through March 21, 1761

Page 1.
Eskridge to Lowe Assignment
This assignment witness Robert Eskridge of the County of Richmond, planter in consideration of 8 pounds and 12 shillings current money of Virginia paid by Richard Lowe of the County of Westmoreland, Planter has assigned, transfer and set over by these presents all that land lying in Yeocomico Neck in the County of Westmoreland which his mother Abigail Eskridge then a widow made a grant of to him in the year 1747 or thereabouts it being at that time part of her jointure and is supposed to contain 50 acres of land more or less as by deed executed and acknowledged in the said County court recorded thereunto. To have and to hold unto the said Richard Lowe his heirs and assigns from henceforth for and during the natural life of the aforesaid Abigail his mother as mentioned and confirm by the aforesaid deed. In witness whereof the said parties to these presents have set their hands and seals this 27th day of April 1756.
Signed sealed and delivered   Robert Eskridge
in the presence of   Richard Lowe
James Clark
John Bailey
Samuel Eskridge
Westmoreland Sct. At a Court held for the said County the 27th day of April 1756 Robert Eskridge came into Court and personally acknowledged this assignment of land and the receipt thereon endorsed by him passed to Richard Lowe to be his proper act and deed which on motion of the said Lowe were ordered to be recorded.
Recorded the fifth day of May 1756   Test
                                      George Lee CCW

Page 2.
Jeffries to Eskridge Indenture
This indenture made the 17th day of November 1756 between Lettice Jeffreys {Jeffries} of Cople Parish in the county of [Westmoreland of the one] part and George Eskridge of the same [Parish of the other] part. Witnesseth [that in consideration of £50] money of Virginia paid by George Eskridge has sold all her right and title being one moiety containing 50 acres being part of a tract of land containing 100 acres be the same more or less which fell to me and my sister Cisley Jeffreys by the death of my brother Edmund Jeffreys, deceased and being now in possession of John Fisher my father-in-law. Scituate lying and being in Yeocomico Neck and bounded by the land of Capt. Peter Rust, Mr. Stephen Bailey and my uncle George Jeffreys land in the Parish and County aforesaid; In witness whereof the said Lettice Jeffreys has set her hand and seal the day and year first above written.
Signed sealed and delivered   Lettice Jeffreys (her mark)
in the presence of
Thomas Butler Sr.
Thomas Butler ,Jr.
Catharine McClane (her mark)
Westmoreland Sct; at a Court held for the said County the 25th day of May 1756 this deed together with the livery of seizen and receipt thereon made passed from Lettice Jeffreys to George Eskridge were proved by the oath of Thomas Butler, Sr., Thomas Butler, Jr., and Catharine McClane witnesses thereto and there upon ordered to be recorded
recorded the 28th day of May 1756   Test
                                     George Lee CCW

Page 5.
Jeffries to Eskridge Bond
Know all men by these presents that we Sissee Jeffreys and Lettice Jeffreys and John Fisher of

Westmoreland County and Cople Parish are held and bounds by these presents to George Eskridge of the county and Parish aforesaid and to his heirs in the full and just some of £100 money of Great Britain this 22nd day of November 1755.

The condition of the above obligation is such that if the above bound Sissee Jeffreys do when she arrives to the age of 21 years make over and convey to the above named George Eskridge or to his heirs part of that tract of land lying in Westmoreland [in Yeocomico] Neck which George Jeffreys gave to his[son Edmond], father to the said Sissee Jeffriss [missing page] without fraud or delay after she arrives to the age in the above obligation to be void and of no effect otherwise to stand and remain in full force strength and virtue in law.

Signed sealed and delivered   Sissee Jeffriss (her mark)
in the presence of us   Lettice Jeffriss (her mark)
Thomas Butler Sr.   John Fisher (his mark)
Thomas Butler, Jr.
William Moore (his mark)

Westmoreland Sct. At a Court held for the said County the 25th day of May 1756 this bond for performance of covenants passed from Sissee Jeffriss, Lettice Jeffriss and John Fisher to George Eskridge was proved by the oaths of Thomas Butler, Sr., Thomas Butler, Jr., and William Moore witnesses thereto and thereupon ordered to be recorded

                                Test
Recorded the 28th day of May 1756   George Lee CCW

Page 6.
Jeffries to Eskridge Arbitration Bond
Know all men by these presents that I George Jeffries of the Parish of Cople and County of Westmoreland am held and firmly [bound] unto George Eskridge of the same Parish and county in the sum of two hundred pounds current money of Virginia this [x] day of April 1756

Whereas a certain [missing] ... The above George Jeffries and George Eskridge [missing] ... property of a certain parcel of land [missing] ... above said Parish and county [missing] by deed [missing] ... Edmond Jeffries his [missing] date the [missing] Dom 1733. By the said deed may appear and afterwards purchased by the said George Eskridge from the heirs of the said Edmund Jeffries. Now to prevent troublesome and expensive law suits concerning the title & inheritance of the said land, the said George Jeffries and George Eskridge of this date mutually and indifferently elected and made choice of Mr. Daniel Tebbs & Mr. Robert Clark by their award in writing duly made and indented under their hands and seals finally to arbitrate and determine the aforesaid right and title of the land between the date hereof and the 10th day of May next.

Now the condition of the above obligation is such that if the above bounded George Jeffries do well and truly stand to and abide the ward and determination of the arbitration then this obligation to be void, otherwise to remain in full force and virtue.   George Jeffries

Sealed and Delivered in the presence of
G. Rust, Vincent Cox, John Brown

Westmoreland Sct. At a court held for the said county the 25th day of May 1756 this arbitration bond passed from George Jeffries to George Eskridge was proved by the oaths of George Rust, Vincent Cox, and John Brown witnesses thereto and thereupon ordered to be recorded.
Recorded the 28th day of May 1756   Test: George Lee CCW

Page 8.
Jeffries vs Eskridge Award
Whereas [George Jeffries] County of Westmoreland & Parish of Cople and [George Eskridge] county and Parish aforesaid have bound them to [missing] him of 200 pounds current money of [Virginia] of us [missing] subscribers dated the tenth [missing] of Mr. Thomas Bennett, Jr., and having all papers and evidences laid before us and hearing all allegations and maturely considering the whole, we find and award that George Jeffries by deed of gift bearing date 25th June 1733 conveyed to his brother Edmund Jeffries a certain tract of land in Yeocomico being one hundred acres or thereabouts to the heirs male of the said Edmund and their heirs forever. We find the right of the said land vested in George Eskridge by purchasing it of Lettice Jeffries and Sissey Jeffries

the daughters of Edmund Jeffries & heirs of Edmund Jeffries their brother.
Given under our hands and seals this 8th day of May 1756
Robert Clarke
Daniel Tebbs
Westmoreland Sct. At a court held for the same county the 25th day of May 1756, this award and determination between George Jeffries and George Eskridge concerning the inheritance of a certain parcel of land was returned into court under the hands of Robert Clarke and Daniel Tebbs and ordered to be recorded.   Test
Recorded the 28th day of May 1756   George Lee CCW

Page 8.
Mothershead's Will
In the name of God Amen, the 25th day of March in the year of our Lord 1756. I Charles Mothershead of the Parish of Washington in the County of Westmoreland being in a poor and low state of health but of good memory, do make this my last will and testament in manner and form as follows;
Item I give and bequeath unto my sister [missing] Negroes Moll, Hannah [missing] natural life and after her death equally divided between my cousin Elizabeth Jeams [James] and my cousin Thomas Jeams [James].
Item I give and bequeath unto my brother-in-law Thomas James everything else that I am master of and all rights and property that belongs to me.
Lastly, I do order constitute and appoint my brother-in-law Thomas James my whole and sole executor of this my land will and testament.
In witness whereof I have hereunto set my hand and fixed my seal this 12th day of April 1756.
Signed in the presence of us   Charles Mothershead
Test, Thomas Wright, John Bulger
Westmoreland Sct. At a court held for the said county the 25th day of May 1756 this will was presented unto court by Thomas James the executor: the same was also proved by Thomas Wright and John Bulger witnesses thereto and thereupon ordered to be recorded. And on motion of the said executor certificate is granted him for obtaining a probate thereof in due form.
Recorded the 28th day of May 1756   Test: George Lee CCW

Page 10.
Sanford to Sanford Arbitration Bond & Award
Know all men by these presents that I Augustine Sanford am held and firmly bound and indented to John Sanford in the full and just sum of 100 pounds current money this 21st day of April 1756. Whereas there is a certain dispute and controversy between Augustine Sanford and John Sanford concerning the division of the lands between them and they have agreed to refer the dispute to Major Thomas Chilton, Mr. John Bushrod and Capt. Wharton Ransdell indifferently named elected and chosen to arbitrate award judge and determine the same. Now the condition of the above obligation is such that if the above bound Augustine Sanford to stand to and abide to the award judgment and final determination of the above recited arbitration and in all things do well and truly observe perform fulfill accomplish and keep those conditions the above allegations is to be void and of non-effect otherwise to stand and remain in full force power and virtue.
Signed sealed and delivered   Augustine Sanford
in the presence of us
Tiperus Degge, Mary Degge (her mark)
We ye subscribers being mutually chosen to settle the bounds of land between John Sanford and Augustine Sanford are of opinion ye tract of land devised by Robert Sanford to his two sons Robert Sanford and John Sanford [missing]... Without any regard to a deed of gift [missing]... Made by Robert Sanford the elder to [missing]...
to [missing]... Bushrod
to [missing]... Ransdell
to [missing]... Chilton
Westmoreland Sct. At a Court held for the said County the 25th day of May 1756 this arbitration

Westmoreland County, Virginia Deeds & Wills DB13, 1756-1761

Bond pass from Augustine Sanford to John Sanford and was proved by the oath of Tiperus Degge a witness to it which together with the award endorsed thereon under the hand of John Bushrod, Wharton Ransdell and Thomas Chilton, Gent., was ordered to be recorded.
Recorded 28th day of May 1756   Test
George Lee CCW

Page 11.
Newton to Cole Lease
This Indenture made this 1st day of September 1755 between John Newton of Westmoreland County, Gent., of the one part and Morris Cole of the same county, shoemaker of the other part. Witnesseth that the said John Newton in consideration of the rents and covenants hereafter mentioned on the part of Morris Cole to be paid or performed hath demised granted let and to farm let and by these presents does demise grant let and to farm let unto the said Morris Cole one messuage tenement and tract of land containing by estimation 40 acres to be the same more or less situated lying and being in Yeocomico Neck and the County of Westmoreland and bounded as following. vizt; beginning at the mouth of a run making out of Rotack [Rotank] Creek commonly called Clayton's run [alias Bonham's Creek] running thence up the said run to several courses and meanders thereof to the land of Daniel McCarty, deceased thence with the said McCarthy's line to Rotack [Rotank] Creek thence down the said creek the several courses and meanders thereof to the beginning together with all houses edifices, orchards gardens pastures, woods underwoods profits commodities hereditaments and appurtenances whatsoever belonging or any wise appertaining to the same except all mines and minerals. To have the said messuage, tenement [missing] of land with the appurtenances [missing] before excepted [missing] for and during [missing] lives of [missing] Cole his wife or the longest liver of them. Yielding and paying yearly during the term aforesaid unto John Newton his heirs or assigns on the 10th day of December the full sum of 3 pounds 4 shillings and 6 pence current money of Virginia. The first of which payments to commence and become due on the 10th day December 1756. In witness whereof the parties above mentioned have interchangeably set their hands and seals the day and date above written.
John Newton
Signed sealed and delivered in presence of   Morris Cole
Rodham Pritchett
Stephen Self, Thomas Clayton
Westmoreland Sct. At a Court held for the said County the 30th day of March 1756 this lease for lives passed from John Newton, Gent., to Morris Cole was proved by the oath of Stephen Self one of the witnesses thereto and ordered to be lodged for further proof.
Test: George Lee CCW
Westmoreland Sct. At a Court held for the said County 25th May 1756 this lease was further proved by the oath of Rodham Pritchett another witness thereto and hereupon ordered to be recorded
Recorded the fourth day of June 1756   Test: George Lee CCW

Page 14.
Lee to Tebbs Arbitration and Award
Know all men by these presents that I Richard Lee of the Parish of Cople and the County of Westmoreland, Esq. am held and firmly bound unto William Tebbs of the Parish of Dettingen and the County of Prince William, Gent., in the sum of £300 this 18th day of June 1756.
The condition of the above obligation is such that whereas there is now depending in the General Court of this colony two lawsuits one brought by the said Tebbs and the other in ejectment for a certain piece and tract of land held by one Henry Wiggington, deceased which said land is now in the possession of the said Lee and now in dispute situated in the Parish of Cople and the County of Westmoreland and the other lawsuit being brought by the said Richard Lee against the said William Tebbs and in order to settle things to right a final determination we the said Richard Lee and William Tebbs have now mutually chosen Henry Lee of the County of Prince William, Esq. and Daniel Tebbs of the County of Westmoreland, Gent., such convenient time and place as both the said land Tebbs shall agree to me sometime between the date hereof and the last day of August

Page 13

next in order to arbitrate the same. The said parties agreeing to standby by such arbitration and determination each party to standby and abide by the said award under the hands and seals of said arbitrators so chosen and forever after to be a ban against all claimants whatsoever in the above obligation to be void or else to remain in full force power and virtue.
Signed sealed and delivered   Richard Lee
in the presence of us
Richard Henry Lee, Joseph Lane
James Woodson
Westmoreland Sct. At a Court held for the said County the 29th day of June 1756 this Arbitration Bond passed from Richard Lee Esq. to William Tebbs, Gent., was presented into Court by the said Tebbs and on his motion is admitted to record
Test: George Lee CCW
Recorded the 14th day of July 1756
Pursuant to certain bonds entered into this day by Richard Lee of the County of Westmoreland Esq. and William Tebbs of the County of Prince William Gent., for settling of a lawsuit depending in the General Court between the parties 117 acres of land situated in the Parish of Cople and County of Westmoreland [missing] to Richard Jackson and Willoughby Allerton's land the [missing]... being formerly in the possession of Henry Wiggington, deceased [missing] seizen and possession of the said Richard Lee; and also the [missing] by the said Richard Lee, plaintiff against the said William Tebbs defendant [missing] the same both which suits are now depending and undetermined. And the said Richard Lee and William Tebbs having mutually and indifferently chosen us the subscribers as umpires and arbitrators to settle the said controversy and disputes arising on the aforesaid suits. On consideration of the several witnesses produced to us and examined into the respective titles to the same lands we do arbitrate award and determine that the title of the aforesaid 117 acres of land is in the said William Tebbs therefore according to the tenure of the aforesaid bonds we do award that the said Lee pay unto the said Tebbs 101 pounds current money for his right to the same lands and that the said Tebbs whenever hereafter demanded or required by the said Richard Lee make or do and execute good and sufficient deed or deeds for conveying the inheritance and fee simple estate of the same lands to the said Lee. And we do further award that the aforesaid two suits be dismissed and the said Lee do pay unto the said Tebbs the legal costs in prosecuting and defending the same. Given under our hands and seals this 18th day of June 1756
Henry Lee
Daniel Tebbs
Westmoreland Sct. At a Court held for the said County the 29th day of June 1756 this award and determination under the hands of Henry Lee, Esq. and Daniel Tebbs, Gent., between Richard Lee, Esq. and William Tebbs, Gent., was presented into Court by the said Tebbs and on his motion admitted to record
Recorded the 14th day July 1756   Test: George Lee CCW

Page 17.
Stapleton & wife to Davis Indenture
This indenture made this 10th day of December 1755 between Thomas Stapleton and Elizabeth Stapleton his wife of Dettingen Parish in the county of Prince William of the one part and Hugh Davis of the Parish of Cople and County of Westmoreland of the other part. Witnesseth that Thomas Stapleton and Elizabeth his wife in consideration of 25 pounds current money have sold unto Hugh Davis a parcel of land in Westmoreland county containing 100 acres more or less being the land the said Thomas Stapleton purchased of one James Habron together with all the houses, edifices, buildings, orchards, feedings, pastures, meadows, woods, swamps, marshes and premises with the appurtenances to the said land now bargained and sold. In witness whereof we the said Thomas & Elizabeth have hereunto set their hands and seals the day and year above written.
Signed Sealed and   Thomas Stapleton (his mark)
Delivered in the presence of us   Elizabeth Stapleton (her mark)
Richard Lee, Joseph Lane

[Francis Farrell]
[Francis] Callis
James [Courtney]
James Woodson
Westmoreland Sct. At a court held for the said county the 29th day of June 1756, this deed together with the livery of seisin and receipts thereon endorsed passed from Thomas Stapleton and Elizabeth his wife to Hugh Davis were all proved by the oaths, Richard Lee, Joseph Lane and James Courtney, three of the witnesses thereto and thereupon ordered to be recorded.
Recorded the 15th day of July 1756   Test: George Lee CCW

Page 17.
Stapleton's wife to Davis Privy Examination
To Henry Lee, Bertrand Ewell and John Baylis of the county of Prince William, Gent., Greeting. Whereas [Thomas] Stapleton and Elizabeth his wife of the Parish of Dettingen in the county of Prince William by their Indenture bearing date 10th day of December [1755] hath conveyed unto Hugh Davis of the County of Westmoreland the fee simple estate of 100 acres of land (more or less) being in Cople Parish and the County of Westmoreland and whereas Elizabeth cannot conveniently travel to our court in Westmoreland County to make acknowledgement we command that you do personally go to the said Elizabeth and receive her acknowledgment without his persuasion or threats. Witness George Lee clerk of said County of Westmoreland the 12th day of December 1755.
Prince William Sct. Pursuant to the written dedimus to us directed we have examined Elizabeth Stapleton wife of Thomas Stapleton separate and apart from him who acknowledged her right of dower in the lands conveyed to Hugh Davis and consents the said deed may be admitted to record in Westmoreland County court. Given under our hand and seal this 24th of May 1756
Henry Lee
John Baylis
Westmoreland Sct. At a Court held for the county 29th June 1756 this commission for the examination of Elizabeth Stapleton wife of Thomas Stapleton relinquishing her right of dower and thirds in the land sold and conveyed to Hugh Davis is ordered to be recorded this 15th day of [July 1756]. CCW

Page 20.
Harrison to Harrison Indenture
This indenture made the 18th day of February 1756 between Samuel Harrison of the Parish of Cople and the County of Westmoreland of the one part and George Harrison of the Parish of St. Stephen's and the County of Northumberland of the other part. Witnesseth that the said Samuel Harrison in consideration of 700 pounds of tobacco in hand paid by the said George Harrison has sold all that tract or parcel or dividend of land situate in the Parish of Cople and the County of Westmoreland it being about 20 acres more or less bounded as followeth. vizt; beginning at a marked hickory the North corner tree between the said George Harrison and the lands of Headley running South to a gully thence down the said gully the head of a branch then down the said branch water and water course to a line of the said Samuel Harrison and Brown thence along said line North to the land of Hammock now in the possession of the said George Harrison, the said land being part of a tract of land patent by George Harrison as by patent [no date]. In witness whereof the parties first within named as interchangeably set his hand and seal the day and year above mentioned. Signed Samuel Harrison
Signed Sealed and delivered in presence of us.
Daniel Harrison, John Short, Darkes Harrison, witnesses
Westmoreland Sct. At a Court held for the said County the 29 June 1756 Samuel Harrison came into Court and personally acknowledged this deed with the livery [& seizen] made of him passed to George Harrison to be his proper [missing] on motion of the said George were admitted to record
Recorded the 15th day of July 1756   Test: George Lee CCW

Page 22.

Bayne to Quisenberry Indenture

This indenture made in the 29th year of the reign of our Sovereign Lord George the Second King of Great Britain France & Ireland King Defender of the Faith; between John Bayn of the County of Westmoreland and Parish of Washington on the one part and William Quesenberry Sr. of the county and Parish aforesaid of the other part. Now this indenture witnesseth that in consideration of one shilling sterling money paid by William Quesenberry at or upon the last day of December yearly during his natural life has given granted & leased to him all that piece of land whereon he now lives (during his life) containing 469 acres of land which bounds will appear by a deed bearing date the 10th day of June 1756 by William Quesenberry Sr. to John Bayne. As witnesseth my hand and seal this 27th day of June 1756   John Bayn

Signed Sealed & delivered in the presence of us
Wm Bridges
Richard Bayn

Westmoreland Sct. At a court held for the said county the 29th day of June 1756 John Bayn came into court and personally acknowledged this lease for lives by him to William Quesenberry to be his proper act and deed and ordered to be recorded.
Recorded the [date missing] Test: George Lee CCW

Page 23.
Roberson's [Robinson] Will

I Thomas Roberson [Robinson] of the County of Westmoreland and Parish of Cople being weak of body but of perfect mind and memory

Item I give and bequeath unto my loving wife Anne Robinson all my whole estate during her life.
Item I give my son Richard Roberson one shilling.
Item I give to my grandson John Roberson, Thomas Roberson's son one cow and calf after my wife's decease.
Item I give unto my grandson Thomas Redman Roberson one feather bed after my wife's decease.
Item I give unto my three sons William Roberson, John Roberson and James Roberson my land to be equally divided after my wife's decease.
Item I constitute and appoint my wife Anne Roberson my Executor of this my last will.

Test: Gerard Hutt Sr.   Thomas Roberson (his mark)
        Gerard Hutt, Jr.

Westmoreland Sct. At a court held for the said county the 29th Day of June 1756 this will was presented into court by Anne Roberson the relict of the decedent and executrix who made oath thereto and the same time proved by the oath of Gerard Hutt, Sr., and Gerard Hutt, Jr., witnesses thereto and ordered to be recorded and on the motion of said executrix and her performing what the law in such cases requires a certificate is granted her for obtaining a probate thereof in due form.
Recorded the 16th day of July 1756   Test: George Lee CCW

Page 24.
Bennett & Wife Indenture to Corbin and Privy Examination

This indenture made this 27th day of August 1756 between Thomas Bennett and Elizabeth Bennett his wife of the Parish of Cople and the County of Westmoreland of one part and Gawin Corbin, Gent., of the Parish and county aforesaid of the other part. Witnesseth that Thomas Bennett and Elizabeth his wife in consideration of 35 pounds paid by Gawin Corbin has sold a tract of land situated upon Yeocomico Creek in the said Parish of Cople and County of Westmoreland containing 41 acres and bounded as follows; beginning at a small red oak at the side of Vincent Rust's Spring Branch and the said rest line thence along the line of marked trees that divides the land from Rust's South 41° 30 poles East 148 poles to a small pine standing on the side of Yeocomico River alias Flints Mill Creek on a pond near Rust's Warehouses thence down the said watercourse northeasterly to the mouth of a cove of the said river thence up the said cove and Spring Branch including all the dried land to the beginning together with all houses outhouses gardens orchards woods ways waters profits and advantages whatsoever. In witness whereof the said Thomas Bennett and Elizabeth his wife have hereunto set their hands and seals this day and

year above written.
Signed Sealed and delivered Thomas Bennett
In the presence of Elizabeth Bennett (her mark)
James Steptoe, Thomas Simpson
Daniel Tebbs, Jr., Richard Lee
Samuel Oldham

Westmoreland Sct. At a Court held for the said County this deed (missing) endorsed passed (missing) Gawin Corbin and were proved by the oath of James Steptoe, Richard Lee and Daniel Tebbs, Jr., three of the witnesses thereto also the livery and seizen proved by the said step two and the and thereupon ordered to be recorded

Recorded the first day of October 1756 Test: George Lee CCW

Westmoreland Sct. By virtue of a commission to us directed to take the personal examination of [Elizabeth] Bennett touching her right of dower to the aforesaid deed bearing date 27th August 1756 we have examined the said Elizabeth apart from her husband Thomas Bennett and she acknowledged her right of dower to the 41 acres of land of her free will. Given under our hands and seals this 28th day of August 1756
Samuel Oldham
Richard Lee

Westmoreland Sct. At a court held for the said county the 28th day of September 1756 this commission for the private examination of Elizabeth Bennett wife of Thomas Bennett for relinquishing her right of dower and thirds to the lands sold to Gawin Corbin.
Recorded this 1st day of October 1756 Test: George Lee CCW

Page 28.
Awbrey's Will
In the name of God Amen, I Chandler Awbrey of the County of Westmoreland and Parish of Cople, planter being sick and weak of body but of sound mind and memory do make this my last will and testament in manner and form following.
In the first place I give my body to the earth from whence it came.
Item I order my body to be buried at the discretion of my executors hereafter named.
Item I order all my just debts be first paid.
Item I give and bequest all my land to my son James Sorrell Awbrey and his heirs forever but if my said son should die before he arrives to the age of 21 years or without heirs of his body lawfully begotten, I give my land and plantation whereon I now live to my daughter [[missing] Awbrey and her heirs
Item I give [missing] estate to be kept together until my eldest daughter arrives at the age of 18 years or days of marriage and then a division to be made among my children and is my further will and desire that my wife's dower Negroes be equally divided among my children when she dies.
Item I give and bequeath to my wife Elizabeth Awbrey what the law gives her and the horse she generally rides in, the saddle and bridle and mourning ring of 20 shillings Sterling value and in full of her dower.
It is my will and desire that my wife should take her thirds out of my lands upon the plantation were I now live
Item I give and bequeath to my sister Hannah McAuley the suit of mourning.
Item I give and bequeath to my niece Mary McAuley a suit of mourning.
Item I give and bequeath to Mrs. Martha Atwell a suit of mourning.
Item I give and bequeath unto Mrs. Elizabeth Atwell a suit of mourning.
Item I give and bequeath to Miss Sarah Atwell a a suit of mourning.
Item it is my will and desire that my children be educated and maintained out of my estate suitable to their situations.
Lastly, I do constitute and appoint my wife friends Richard Lee Esq., Mr. Daniel Tebbs and Mr. Spencer Ariss executors and my wife Elizabeth Awbrey executrix of this my last will and testament. In witness whereof I have hereunto set my hand and seal this ninth day of December in the year of our Lord Christ 1755.
Chandler Awbrey

The last will and testament of Chandler Awbrey
Signed sealed and delivered and published in the presence of
Richard Lee, Gabriel Johnston, Henry Allison, James Balfour
Westmoreland Sct. At a Court held for the said County on the 28th day of September 1756 this will was presented into Court by Elizabeth Awbrey (the relict of the deceased) and Richard Lee, Esq. two of the executors therein named who made oath thereto and the same being also proved by the oath of Richard Lee, Henry Allison and James Balfour three the witnesses thereto who ordered to be recorded and on motion of the said executors and their performing what the law in such cases require a certificate is granted them for obtaining [probate] thereof in due form
Test: George Lee CCW

Page 30.
Lane to Lane Deed of Gift
This indenture made this 28th day of September 1756 between William Lane, Sr of Cople Parish and Westmoreland County of one part and Joseph Lane son of said William Lane of the same county and Parish of the other part. Witnesseth that William Lane in consideration of the natural love and affection with the hath unto the said Joseph Lane and in consideration for the better maintenance and livelihood of him and the sum of five shillings has confirmed unto the said Joseph Lane his heirs and assigns forever all that tract of land which I purchased of William Walker and Felicity Walker his wife containing 150 acres and lying by Mr. Carter's Double Mill in the same County and all and singular the houses edifices buildings Barnes stables courts gardens orchards feedings woods underwoods commons common of pasture, ways paths passages waters and watercourses easements profits commodities advantages. Hereditaments and appurtenances whatsoever
Westmoreland Sct. At a court held for said county the 28th day of Sept 1756 William Lane came into court and personally acknowledged this deed of gift to his son Joseph Lane to be his proper act and deed which on the motion of the said Joseph was ordered to be recorded.
Recorded the 1st day of October 1756   George Lee, CCW

Page 31.
Tidwell to Tidwell Deed of Gift
This indenture made this 30th day of August 1756 between Robert Tidwell of Cople Parish and Westmoreland County of the one part and William Carr Tidwell of the same Parish & county son of the said Robert Tidwell, in consideration of the natural love and affection he hath unto William Carr Tidwell and in consideration of the better maintenance and livelihood hath given the land in Machodoc Neck purchased of [Isaac Allerton by deed dated 29 July 1734] containing 173 acres which land my son now lives on where he is to have the half of said tract laid off and all and singular the houses edifices buildings barnes stables courts garden orchards feedings woods underwoods commons, common pastures, ways paths passages water watercourses easements profits commodities advantages hereditaments and appurtenances only reserving that the said Robert Tidwell shall have the use of any of the timber on any part of said land.
Robert Tidwell (his mark)
Westmoreland Sct. At a Court held for said County the 28th day of September 1756 this deed of gift passed from Robert Tidwell to his son William Carr Tidwell and was proved by the oaths of Bennett Abraham Garner and Joseph Lane witnesses thereto and thereupon ordered to be recorded
Recorded the second day of October 1756   Test: George Lee CCW

Page 33.
Price's will
in the name of God Amen. I Evan Price of Westmoreland County being in perfect senses and memory do ordain this my last will and testament in manner and form following
First, I give Virlinda Balthrop one grey mare and two gold rings that she now possesses in lieu of any claim she has against me on my estate to be in full of all accounts
Secondly, I give to my brother John Price all my wearing clothes, my saddle and bridle and no more.

Westmoreland County, Virginia Deeds & Wills DB13, 1756-1761

Thirdly, my will is that all the rest of the estate be it of what nature or property soever I lend to my mother Sarah Price and my sisters Mary Price and Grace Price and the profits of the same to be equally divided between them yearly for their support and further my will is that either of them should marry, then the married one to have no claim to any part of my estate yearly profits but them that keep themselves single till their death to keep the estate and make use of the profits for their support.

Fourthly, my will is that after they marry or death of my mother and two sisters, I give my whole estate of Negroes (not before given) to my uncle Henry Field and his heirs forever but in case my brother John Price any [missing] should make a second marriage, I [missing] to me [missing] Field and give the whole of my estate not [missing] Price forever as if my uncle had not been before mentioned.

Fifthly and lastly, I appoint my mother Sarah Price my whole and sole executrix to this my last will. of November 1755

Signed Sealed and delivered in presence of   Evan Price
James Berryman
Frankling Lathukem

Westmoreland Sct. At a court held for the said County the 28th day of September 1756 this world presented into Court by Sarah Price the executrix therein named who made oath thereto and being proved by the witnesses was ordered to be recorded and on the motion of said executrix and her performing which the law in such cases require a certificate is granted her for obtaining a probate in due form.

Recorded the second day of October 1756   George Lee CCW

Page 34.
Moxley to Moxley Deed of Gift
Know all men by these presents that I Richard Moxley in the County of Westmoreland in consideration of the natural love and affection which I have and unto my son Richard Moxley of said county has confirmed unto him his heirs and assigns all that tract of land that I bought of Nicholas Minor, Jr., which he bought of Samuel Moxley by estimation 70 acres.

Sealed and delivered in presence of us   Richard Moxley
Francis Lightfoot Lee
Thomas Chilton, Jr.
Edward Moxley

Westmoreland Sct. At a court held for the said county the 28th day of September 1756 Richard Moxley came into court and personally acknowledged this deed of Gift by him passed to his son Richard Moxley to be his act and deed which on motion of said Richard was ordered to be Recorded

Recorded this 2nd day of October 1756   Test: George Lee CCW

Page 36.
Moxley to Moxley Deed of Gift
Know all men by these presents that I Richard Moxley in the County of Westmoreland in consideration of the natural love and affection which I have and unto my son Edward Moxley of said county has confirmed unto him his heirs and assigns all that tract of land that I bought of Capt. Richard Sanford by estimation 150 acres.   Richard Moxley

Sealed and delivered in presence of us
Francis Lightfoot Lee
Thomas Spence

Westmoreland Sct. At a court held for the said county the 28th day of September 1756 Richard Moxley came into court and personally acknowledged this deed of Gift by him passed to his son Edward Moxley to be his act and deed which on motion of said Richard was ordered to be recorded

Recorded this 2nd day of October 1756   Test: George Lee CCW

Page 37.
Roe's Will

Westmoreland County, Virginia Deeds & Wills DB13, 1756-1761

I Bunch Roe of ye County of Westmoreland & Parish of Washington do make my will and testament in manner and form following

Item I give to my nephew William Roe two Negroes Bob & Jem and his heirs forever

Item I give to Amy Pritchett by best bed and furniture & my bay horse.

Item I give my horse named Popin to Susan Baker.

Item my will is that Amy Pritchett have her wages for 1755 as also for the present year 1756, that is 1200 pounds crop tobacco and two pair of shoes.

Item my desire is that the remains of my personal estate, crop, negroes &c be sold to the highest bidder and (after my debts are paid) to be equally divided amongst Thomas Whiting's children.

Item I appoint my brother Henry Roe, William Monroe & John Weedon as executors.

If John Weedon will be concerned about my estate, my desire is he be paid five years rent for selling and receiving.

Given under my hand this 26th day of July 1756   Bunch Roe (his mark)

Signed in presence of
William Tyler (his mark)
James Bankhead
John Jordan (his mark)

N.B. my will further is that Butler Baker have my saddle & bridle along with the horse Popin.

Item that Amy Pritchett have the chest that she has now in use.

Item that the negroes shall remain and be employed in tending my crop till finished

As witness my hand   Bunch Roe (his mark)

Signed in presence of
James Bankhead
John Jordan (his mark)

Westmoreland Sct. At a court held for the said county the 28th day of September 1756 this will and codicil were presented into court by Henry Roe one of the executors who made oath thereto and being proved by James Bankhead and John Jordan witness to them were ordered to be recorded and on the motion of the said executor and his performing what is usual in such cases certificate is granted him for obtaining a probate thereof in due form.

Recorded the 4th day of October 1756   George Lee CCW

Page 38.
Claytor's Will
In the name of God Amen, This 27 Day of December 1750. I Thomas Claytor of the Parish of Washington and County of Westmoreland being very sick and weak of body but of perfect and sound mind and memory do make this my las will and testament.

First my soul into the hands of Almighty God and my body I commit to the earth

Imprimis: I give and bequeath unto my eldest son John Claytor five shillings .. [missing] land already, bounded and acknowledged to him and also an equal part of my personal estate except the legacies hereafter specified.

Item I give and bequeath unto my two sons Thomas Claytor and Alvin Claytor a tract of land called the Broad Neck, bounded as follows; beginning at a white oak in the fork of two roads and thence along the line of John Claytor to the line of Nathaniel Mothershead and thence along the said line to a corner tree of Butler land, and thence down to the Miry Branch and up the said branch to the beginning to be equally divided between them and their heirs forever.

I leave the remaining part of my lands for the use of my daughter Elizabeth Claytor during her single life.

Item I give and bequeath unto my two sons William Claytor & Samuel Claytor the said remaining part of my lands (after my daughter Elizabeth Claytor's marriage or death to be equally divided. In case either or both should die without heirs, then such part of their lands to descend to my grandson William Claytor son of John Claytor.

Item I give and bequeath unto my daughter Elizabeth Claytor a feather bed and furniture whereon I used to lie and her choice of two cows and calves. Likewise, my best iron pot and the best frying pan, my gray mare, servant man Thomas Jerwood during his servitude, my will is that he be remitted one year of his time. Also, the provision of corn and wheat now in the house.

Page 20

Westmoreland County, Virginia Deeds & Wills DB13, 1756-1761

Item I give unto my daughter Anne Claytor a large looking glass.
Item My will and desire is that my grandson William Claytor son of John Claytor shall have five years schooling and to be paid for it out of my estate.
Item my will and desire is that the remaining part of my estate (after the aforementioned legacies and debts are discharged) shall be equally divided amongst my seven children.
Lastly I ordain constitute and appoint my two sons Thomas Claytor and Alvin Claytor and my daughter Elizabeth Claytor executors and executrix of this my land will and testament.
Signed Sealed published & delivered in the presence of us   Thomas Claytor (his mark)
John Elliott
Nathaniel Mothershead
Christopher Quisenbury
John Carter
Christopher Collins
Westmoreland Sct. At a court held for the said county the 28th day of September 1756 this will was presented into court by Thomas Claytor and Elizabeth Claytor two of the Executors therein named who made oath thereto and being proved by the oath of Nathaniel Mothershead, John Carter and Christopher Collins three of the witnesses to it was ordered to be recorded and on the motion on the said executors and them performing what the law in such cases require, certificate is granted them for obtaining a probate thereof in due form.
Recorded the 4th day of October 1756   Test: George Lee CCW

Page 40.
Ashton to Storke Privy Examination
To John Martin, James Berryman and Richard Henry Lee of Westmoreland County greetings. Whereas Henry Ashton of the aforesaid county and Jane Ashton his wife by their indenture of feoffment dated 26th day of April 1756 has conveyed unto John Storke, Gent., of the same county, the fee simple estate of 300 acres of land lying in the Parish of Cople and County of Westmoreland. And whereas Jane cannot conveniently travel to our county court to acknowledge the conveyance, we therefore command you or any two of you to personally receive her acknowledgement.
Witness
George Lee Clerk of our said county court the 1st day of July 1756.
Westmoreland Sct. In obedience to a commission, we have privately examined Jane Ashton apart from her husband and she acknowledged the right of that conveyance. Given under our hands and seals this 12th day of October 1756.
John Martin
James Berryman
Westmoreland Sct. At a court held for the said county the 26th day of October 1756 this commission for the examination of Jane Ashton wife of Henry Ashton for relinquishing her right of dower and thirds to the lands sold to John Storke was ordered to be recorded.
Recorded the 2nd day of November 1756   Test: George Lee CCW

Page 41.
Pritchett from Self Indenture
This indenture made this 26 day of April 1756 between William Self of Cople Parish and Westmoreland County of one part and Rodham Pritchett of the same Parish and county of the other part. Witnesseth that William Self in consideration of 33 pounds current money of Virginia paid by Rodham Pritchett has sold all that piece of land below the main road containing four acres more or less in the Parish of Cople and is bounded as followeth; vizt; joining upon the land of Presley Cox and upon the land of Thomas Bennett, Jr. and the land of Thomas Self to the road with all and singular its rights, members, jurisdictions and appurtenances. In witness whereof the parties to this presents have interchangeably set their hands and seals the day and year above written.
Signed Sealed and delivered in the presents of us   William Self (his mark)
Fleet Cox, Richard Halliday
George Cox, John Gardner
Westmoreland Sct. At a court held for the said county the 26th May 1756 this deed with the livery of

seizen and receipt thereon made passed from William Self to Rodham Pritchett were all proved by Richard Halliday one of the witnesses to them and ordered to be lodged for further proof.
Test: George Cox CCW
Westmoreland Sct. At a court held for the said county the 25th May 1756 this deed with the livery of seizen and receipt thereon was fully proved by the oaths of Fleet Cox and John Gardner two other witnesses to them and thereupon were ordered to be recorded.
Recorded the 3rd day of November 1756   Test: George Cox CCW

Page 45.
Courtney's Will
In the name of God Amen. I Mary Courtney of the Parish of Cople and County of Westmoreland being sick and weak of body but of good and perfect sense and memory to make this my last will and testament.
Imprimis, I give unto my son Samuel Courtney my best bed and furniture.
Item I give unto my daughter Rosamond Garner all my wearing apparel.
Item I given to my granddaughter Mary Garner one gold ring of 10 shillings value.
And all the remainder of my estate of what nature or kind soever I give and hereafter unto my four sons James Courtney, Leonard Courtney, Samuel Courtney and [Jeremiah Courtney] equally divided amongst them.
And I do hereby constitute and appoint my two sons Leonard Courtney and Jeremiah Courtney to be my executors of this my last will and testament. In witness whereof I hereunto set my hand and seal this 10th day of July 1756   Mary Courtney (her mark)
Signed sealed and delivered in the presence of
Samuel Rust
Peter Mullins, Elizabeth Mullins (her mark)
Westmoreland Sct. At a court held for said County the 26th day of October 1756 this will was presented into Court by Leonard and Jeremiah Courtney the executors therein named who made oath thereto and the same being also proved by Samuel Rust & Peter Mullins two of the witnesses and on motion of said executors and their performing what the law in such cases requires certificate was granted them for obtaining a probate thereof in due form.
Recorded the third day of November 1756   Test: George Lee CCW

Page 46.
Davis to Wroe Indenture
This indenture made 25th day of October 1756 between Joshua Davis of the Parish of Washington and County of Westmoreland, Planter, eldest son and heir of Samuel Davis late of the said county, planter, deceased of the one part and William Wroe of the parish and county aforesaid of the other part. Now whereas John Baker, deceased by lease bearing date January 3, 1756 did the devise, grant set and to farm let unto Thomas English of the said County of Westmoreland, deceased, part of a plantation lying at Attopin Creek in the County aforesaid containing about 150 acres of land. Bounded as follows, vizt; beginning at a marked gum in the mouth of a valley on the side of a wash of Attopin Creek extending thence southeast or thereabouts of the said valley along a line of marked trees un equally standing to a marked walnut on the south side of the main road thence through the wood by the hill commonly called and known by the name of "the Round about Hill" to the back line of the aforesaid John Baker, deceased thence along the said Baker's and John Weedon's line to the aforesaid creek thence down the said creek according to the several meanders thereof to the first beginning. Including all the land and marsh that was formally granted or leased to Thomas English aforesaid. And whereas the late Thomas English said was assigned to the land Samuel Davis who intermarried with Anne Baker the daughter of the said John Baker, deceased and whereas the said John Baker by his last will and testament bearing date 19th day of November 1727 did give and devise unto the said Anne Davis his daughter, the said parcel of land formerly leased to Thomas English for and during her natural life and afterwards to her husband Samuel Davis for two years and afterward to fall to his two sons Butler Baker and John Baker. And whereas the said Anne Davis is now in possession of the said land and the said Samuel Davis did agree to with Butler Baker to purchase all his right and title and interest to the reversion and

Westmoreland County, Virginia Deeds & Wills DB13, 1756-1761

inheritance of the said land and premises as appears by deed bearing date the 26th day of September 1749. Now this indenture witness that in consideration of 25 pounds current money of Virginia paid to Joshua Davis by William Wroe the said Joshua Davis has sold him all his right title and interest to that parcel of land with all appurtenances lying in the parish and County aforesaid and now in possession of Anne Davis.

Signed Sealed and delivered in the presence of   Joshua Davis
Original Wroe, William Craighill,
John Hilton, Archibald Campbell
Augustine Smith, William Edwards
John Martin

Westmoreland Sct. At a Court held for the said County the 26th day of October 1756 this deed and the receipt for consideration thereon was passed from Joshua Davis to William Wroe were proved by the oath of Archibald Campbell, John Martin and William Craig Hill and thereupon ordered to be recorded.
Recorded the 12th day of November 1756   George Lee CCW

Page 50.
Elliott's Will
in the name of God Amen, this 25th day of May 1756 I John Elliott of the Parish of Washington and the County of Westmoreland being very sick and weak of body but of perfect mind and memory do make this my last will and testament

Imprimis, I give unto my beloved wife one Negro girl named Nell to her at her disposal and all my other estate to her and her heirs forever.

Item I give my tract of land lying in Prince William County containing 2700 acres to my three sons William Elliott, Robert Elliott and Augustine Elliott and William and Robert to have 1000 acres each and Augustine 700 acres.

Item I leave my two sons William Elliott and Robert Elliott to Capt. John Rowzee to do for them direct and dispose of them according to his discretion. Whom I likewise constitute make and ordain my sole executor of this my last will and testament.

Signed, Sealed and delivered in presence of   John Elliott
Francis Williams, John Price
Thomas Muse

Westmoreland Sct. At a Court held for the said County the 26th day of October 1756 this will was presented into Court by Elenor Elliott the relict of the decedent which being proved by the oath of John Price and Thomas Muse two of the witnesses, it was admitted to record and it being signified to the court that John Rowzee the executor therein named refuses to take upon himself the burden of the execution thereof; therefore on the motion of the said Elenor Elliott and her performing what the law in such cases requires administrating of all and singular the goods and chattels of the said John Elliott, deceased was in due form granted her.
Recorded the 12th day of November 1756   George Lee CCW

Page 51.
Suggett to Morton Indenture
this indenture made the 13th day of October 1756 between James Suggett of the County of Culpeper and Parish of St. Mark's of the one part and William Morton the County of Westmoreland and Parish of Cople of the other part. Witness that James Suggett in consideration of 16,240 pounds crop tobacco paid by William Morton has sold all that tract of land being in the County of Westmoreland and Parish of Cople containing 150 acres it being the same lands James Suggett purchased from George Lamkin.   James Suggett
in the presence of Daniel [Tebbs], Smith [King],
[William Gilbert]
[Isaac Proctor], [Samuel King (his mark)]
Memorandum, that on the 14th day of October 1756 James Suggett made livery and seizen of the land and appurtenances by delivering turf and twigg and the ring of the doors of the chief mansion house on the land within mentioned unto William Morton.

In the presence of us
Daniel Tebbs, Smith King, William Gilbert, Isaac Proctor, Samuel King (his mark)
Westmoreland Sct. At a Court held for the said County the 30th day of November 1756 this deed with the receipt and livery of seizen thereon made passed from James Suggett to William Morton and being all proved by the oath of Daniel Tebbs, Samuel King and William Gilbert, three of the witnesses.
Recorded the 8th day of December 1756 Test: [no signature]

Page 54.
Middleton's will
In name of God Amen, this 10th day of October 1756 by Benjamin Middleton of the Parish of Cople and the County of Westmoreland being sick and weak of body but of perfect mind and memory make this my last will and testament.
Imprimis, my will and desire is that my loving wife to Jemima Middleton may have the liberty as long as she remains single to live on and occupy my plantation whereon, I now live and after her death or marriage to be sold at public auction together with all my other lands to me belonging by my executors and the purchase thereof I give and bequeath to be equally divided amongst all my children Mary, Alice, Benjamin, James and Elizabeth.
Item And as for my crops made this year my will and desire is that my debts and public dues may be paid out of the same and the remaining purchase thereof, I give and bequeath to the support and maintenance of my family now living on my said plantation.
Item As for all the residue of my estate as Negroes stock and household goods or any other to me belonging I give and bequeath it equally divided between my loving wife to Jemima Middleton, my daughter Mary Brown, my daughter Alice Harrison, my son Benjamin Middleton, my daughter Jane Middleton, and my daughter Elizabeth Middleton, everyone to have an equal part. But in such case that my daughter Mary Brown may have my Negro woman Frank in her part and in case the said Frank should have a child between this and the time of her being appraised my will and desire is that my said daughter may have the child over and above her share and that my daughter Alice Harrison may have my Negro Tony in her share and my daughter Jane may have my Negro Rhoda in her share and that my daughter Elizabeth may have my Negro girl Pegg in her share and my loving wife Jemima to have my sorrel horse called "Wonton" in her share. If any of the said Negroes by their valuation should amount to more than their equal part to whom they were left then they to return and paid to the other of my children proportion so that everyone may have an equal share of my said estate.
Item I also make and ordain to Jeremiah Middleton and William Middleton my executors of this my last will and testament.
Signed Sealed and published and pronounced in the presence of us   Benjamin Middleton
Robert Middleton, G. Rust
Benedict Middleton, Robert Middleton, Jr.
Westmoreland Sct. At a court held for the said County the 30th day of November 1756 this will was presented into Court by Jeremiah Middleton and William Middleton the executors therein named who made oath thereto and being proved by the oath of George Rust, Benedict Middleton and Robert Middleton, Jr., three of the witnesses to it was submitted to record and it is ordered that a certificate be granted the executors for obtaining a probate thereof in due form.
Recorded this 8th day of December 1756   Test: George Lee CCW

Page 56.
Butler's Will
In the name of God Amen, I Thomas Butler of Westmoreland County, planter being much indisposed & sick but of sound mind & memory do make this my last will and testament in manner and form following.
I give unto my son John Butler all my land with the will upon it to him and his heirs and in case he should die before he arrives at the age of 21 and not having lawful heir then I leave the said land and mill to my daughter Elizabeth Butler and her heirs.
I give unto William Jackson my best bed and furniture.

Westmoreland County, Virginia Deeds & Wills DB13, 1756-1761

I give unto Sarah Jackson her choice of one my horses.
I give unto [missing] Jr. [missing] corn & six hogs.
I give unto Anne Butler, Jr. [missing] & schooling, my children
I give all the rest [missing] aforesaid son & daughter, my son paying to my daughter five pounds Virginia currency.
Item, it is my will that my estate shall be appraised and sold which is to be divided between my son and daughter.
And I appoint Anne Butler, Jr. and Thomas Butler, Jr., executors of this my last will and testament.
In witness whereof I have hereunto set my hand and seal this 13th day of August 1756
Test: Thomas Butler (his mark)
James Blair, John Mason
Thomas Taylor
Westmoreland Sct. At a court held for said county this 30th day of November 1756 this will was presented into court by Anne Butler, Jr. one of the executors therein named who made oath thereto and being proved by James Blair and Thomas Taylor two of the witnesses to it (who also made oath that they saw John Mason subscribe it as a witness) was admitted to record. And ordered that a certificate be granted to the said executor for obtaining a probate thereof in due form.
Recorded the 8th day of December 1756   Test: George Lee CCW

Page 57.
Higdon to Butler Mortgage
This indenture made the 14th day of June 1756 between John Higdon of the Parish of Washington and County of Westmoreland, planter of the one part and Laurence Butler of the parish and county aforesaid, Gent., of the other part. Whereas John Higdon was seized and possessed as tenant in fee tail of a certain tract of land lying on Mattox Creek in the parish and county aforesaid containing by estimation 100 acres and being minded to sell and dispose of the same did sue forth a writ in the nature of an Ad Quod Dammum to the sheriff of said County of Westmoreland directed to dock the entail of the said land and premises pursuant to the act of General Assembly in such cases made and provided by virtue of which said writ and inquisition was taken before James Berryman, Gent., Sherriff of the County of Westmoreland [missing] Higdon afterwards by a deed of bargain and [missing] did for a certain [missing] unto Matthew Bayne and his heirs all and singular the said entail with lands and premises with all the appurtenances as by the said deed remaining on record in the General Court of this colony. And whereas the said Matthew Bayne afterwards by deed of bargain and sale reciting the above premises for a certain consideration therein mentioned did reconvey to the said John Higdon and his heirs part of the said land and premises reserving to himself a certain parcel thereof according to a contract and agreement between them. And whereas John Higdon afterwards by deed of bargain and sale for valuable consideration therein mentioned did sell and convey unto Laurence Butler one other parcel of the said land and premises lying on Mattox Creek by particular metes and bounds therein specified. Now this indenture witnesseth that John Higdon in consideration of 19 pounds current money of Virginia paid by Laurence Butler has sold the residue of the said tract of land lying on Mattox Creek. Provided always and upon condition that if the said John Higdon shall well and truly pay to Laurence Butler 19 pounds current money upon the 14th day of October next ensuing then these presents shall cease.   John Higdon
In the presence of
John Lovell, David Craig
James Berryman, John Martin
Westmoreland Sct. At a court held for the said county the 26th day of October 1756, this mortgage passed from John Higdon to Laurence Butler was proved by the oaths of John Lovell and [missing]
Westmoreland Sct. At a court held for the said county the 30th day of October 1756, this mortgage was fully proved by the oath of James Berryman another witness to it and thereupon ordered to be recorded.
Recorded this 8th day of December 1756   Test: George Lee CCW

Page 62.

Harrison to Monroe Privy Examination

To John Martin, James Berryman & John Monroe, Gent., of Westmoreland county, greetings. Whereas Lovell Harrison by his indenture conveyed unto Andrew Monroe, Gent., of the county aforesaid the fee simple inheritance of about 191 acres of land in Washington Parish and the county aforesaid and whereas Hannah Harrison cannot conveniently travel to court to make acknowledgement of her said dower, therefore we do give unto any two of you power to receive her acknowledgement of the indenture and this writ. Witness, George Lee Clerk of our said county court the 31st of October in the xxix th year of our reign.   George Lee CCW

Westmoreland Sct. Pursuant to the above commission to us directed we have examined Hannah Harrison wife of Lovell Harrison who freely and voluntarily acknowledged the same should be recorded.
John Martin
John Monroe
Westmoreland Sct. At a court held for the said county the 22nd February 1757 this commission was returned and ordered to be recorded.
Recorded the 9th day of March 1757   Test: George Lee CCW

Page 62.
Purland's Will

In the name of God Amen, I Matthew Purland and of the County of Westmoreland and Virginia and sick of body but with perfect memory make this my last will and testament.

First I commit my soul into the hands of Almighty God in my body to be decently buried in Richmond Church Yard by my wife that church by Mr. Barnness and put me in my Ghislestin shirt to be buried in.

Item my will is that all my debts be paid between this and Christmas next and all the church and bills and bonds to be called in as soon as possible and sent home to my friend William Woods Taylor at Norwich for my children.

Item my will is that my mare and all my goods be sold and the cash; to my friend Mr. William Woods Taylor in Norwich to be left at Mr. Ben Days at Long's Warehouse in Tavestock Street near Covent Garden, London.

Only my wife's clothes and linen that are in the dale box to be sent home for her daughter according to her desire. I have put a superscription on the box where it is to go.

Item I choose Robert Carter, Esq., Thomas Ludwell Lee, Esq. and Mr. Henry Franks, Doctor. to be sole executors of this my [last] will and testament.

Item my will is after the goods are [missing] paid the gentleman satisfied for their trouble I desire the balance to be sent home to my friends Woods as I have mentioned before.

Given under my hand and seal this ninth day of September 1756.
Signed and sealed in the presence of us   Matthew Purland
Thomas Atwell, John Smith

Westmoreland Sct. At a court held for the said County the 22nd February 1757 this will was proved by the oath of Thomas Atwell and John Smith the witnesses thereto and ordered to be recorded and on the motion of Henry Franks one of the executors therein named and his performing what is usual in such cases a certificate was granted him for obtaining a probate thereof in due form.
Recorded the ninth day of March 1757   Test: George Lee CCW

Page 63.
Bayne vs Bushrod Processioner's Report

Westmoreland Sct. At a court held for the said County the 30th day of March 1756 James Hore one of the churchwardens of Washington Parish presented into Court a Processioner's Report under the hand of John Bulger, Edward Muse and Nathaniel Mothershead. That they processioned the lands of John Bushrod unto a white oak the corner of Matthew Bayne's lands where they were ordered to procession no further by the said Bayne. Whereupon pursuant to the act of assembly in that case provided it is considered by the court that the surveyor of the said County in company with an able jury of freeholders of the vicinage who are no ways concerned in interest or related by affinity or consanguinity to either of the parties, non-liable to any other just exceptions, to be summoned by the sheriff and sworn before Justice of peace for the said County, to go upon the lands in difference between the said Matthew Bayne and John Bushrod on the fourth day of April next, and lay off the bounds in dispute; the sheriff to attend the survey and remove force if any offered and the surveyor to return with a copy of said survey.

Page 64.
Bayne vs Bushrod's Plat & Survey
[Surveyors plat at top of page] Westmoreland to wit: pursuant to an order of the said County Court dated 22nd day of March 1756 made in a stop of processioning by Matthew Bayne against John Bushrod, Gent., in the Parish of Washington I the subscriber in company of a jury sworn according to law and the sheriff of the said county; met on the lands in dispute on the day mentioned in the said order. The plaintiff refusing to survey, then at request of the defendants began at a corner white oak at the letter "A" and run northwest till I came to the run at the letter "B".
Survey 22nd of April. B. Weeks, S. W. Cty

Page 64.
Bayne vs Bushrod Jury Verdict
Westmoreland to wit: Matthew Bayne, plaintiff vs John Bushrod, defendant
In pursuance of an order from the worshipful court of the County aforesaid and whose names are underwritten been impaneled and sworn a jury before Thomas Lee, Gent., and justice for the said County together with the surveyor and sheriff thereof and upon the lands in dispute and the aforesaid plaintiff refusing to survey any part thereof and producing no deeds or other evidence the defendants thereto upon directed us to a white oak proved by the testimony of Humphrey Pope and mentioned in a deed and survey of the said land and ran northwest by two line trees appearing to be anciently marked to a swamp according to the directions in the aforesaid survey and thence along the ancient watercourses on which line the said plaintiff stopped the procession in which we now report to be the true line and have currently marked it. Witness our hands and seals this 22nd day of April 1756

Daniel Neale, Jr.	John Muse
Ben Rust	Lawrence Butler
Nathan Ja[ckson]	John Naughty
John [missing]	Daniel Moxley
[missing]	Edward Sanford
[missing]	George [missing[yne

Westmoreland Sct. At a court continued held for said County the 25th day of February 1757 the Surveyor's Plat, Report and Jury Verdict hereunto annexed in a Stop of Processioning made by Matthew Bayne against John Bushrod was returned into court and pursuant to the act of assembly in such cases made and provided on the motion of the said John Bushrod were admitted to record. Recorded the 9th day of March 1757

Page 65.
Carter vs Garner Processioner's Report
Westmoreland Sct. At a Court held for said County the 25th day of May 1756 the former orders of this court on a return of Thomas Garner and Richard Halliday, processioners certifying that they were stopped on the lane between Robert Carter, Esq. and Abraham Garner, by the said Garner, in the presence of Ransdell, John Crabb and Vincent Garner, for the survey of this County in the company of an able jury of freeholders of the vicinage no ways concerned in interest or related by affinity or consanguinity to either of the parties, non-liable to any other just exceptions, to be summoned by the sheriff and sworn before Justice of peace for the said County, to go upon the lands in difference between the said parties on the 13th day of April and lay off the bounds in dispute and that the surveyor return a copy of such survey to the next court and not being complied with it is therefore now began ordered that the said Sheriff do summons such jury and that they in company of said surveyor due on the third day of June next perform that service and make a like report of their proceedings therein, to next court.
Copy Test   George Lee CCW

Page 66.
Garner vs Carter Surveyors Plat and Survey
[Surveyors plat on page]

Page 67.
Garner vs Carter Jury Verdict
Westmoreland to Wit: Abraham Garner vs Robert Carter, Gent. > Stop in Processioning
In obedience to an order of the said county court dated the 25th day of May 1756 I the subscriber in company of the jury sworn and the sheriff, met on the land in difference on the day mentioned in the said order. First by request of plaintiff began near the mouth of Hurd's Creek at "A" extending up Potomack River N.B.W. 346 pole but at the end of the 300 poles angled to a place where formerly lived one Baugres, tenant of Joseph Hutson under whom the plaintiff claims proved by Richard Browne and John West, and at the end of 346 poles angled to a red oak stump claimed by the plaintiff which bore North 56° East 6° po. 28 links. Thence S.B.E. 58 then was directed by the plaintiff's and jury to angle to Allerton's line to find the corner course which bore S.52° W 65 po, which is laid down by the figures 2.3 [missing] C.S.B.E 170 poles to one of the branches [missing] the plaintiff to begin at corner red oak [missing] figures 5 and six. Then by request of the defendant began at the end of 250 poles in plaintiff's line at the letter "H" crossing a pond and along a line of ancient line trees 320 poles but at the end of 170 poles Thomas Williams being examined said that to the right hand from the river lives one Morris Jolly about 28 years ago was a tenant 21 Robert Carter, Gent., whom this defendant claims under. Then John West being examined said that about 40 years ago Morris Jolly lived at the same place a tenant to one Garner homeless plaintiff claims under. At the end of 320 poles corner in Osmond Crabb's orchard, at the letter "I" thence S.B.E. hundred and 50 poles at the creek near John Crabb's house at the letter "K" which is laid down with blue lines in letters "H", "I" and "K".
Surveyed B. Weeks S. W. Cty
Westmoreland to Wit: in obedience to an order of Court hereunto annexed bearing date 25 May 1756 we the jury being sworn before Richard Jackson, Gent., one of his Majesties Justices for the said County and in company with the surveyor of the said County have met upon the lands according to the said order and proceeded as follows; vizt; beginning at the mouth of Hurd's Creek extending up Potomack River according to the courses of the said patent to a red oak stump standing upon the edge of the bank of the said River proved to be the corner tree of Hurd's patent by the information of Charles Brown, deceased given to Richard Brown about 30 years past and also to John Lathrum about 15 years past, and also to Manley Brown about 20 years past, extending from thence South and by West into the main woods to a marked white oak appearing to us to be a corner tree of Hudson's deed which was a sale out of the said patent which we take to be the true line of Hurd's patent to which line we find for Abraham Garner, plaintiff. Given under our hands and seals this fifth day of June 1756.

John Brown	Daniel Tebbs, foreman
William Lane, Jr.	William Callis
Robert Middleton	Thomas Spence
George Eskridge	Daniel Moxley
Samuel Harrison	James Bailey
John Sanford	[missing] Atwell

Westmoreland Sct. At a court continued and held for the said County the 26th day of February 1757 the surveyor's plat, report and jury verdict hereunto annexed in a stop of processioning made by Abraham Garner against Robert Carter, Esq. were returned into court and pursuant to the act of general assembly in such cases made and provided on the motion of the said Abraham Garner were admitted to record.
Recorded the 10th day of March 1757   Test: George Lee CCW

Page 69.
Bayne to Quesenbury
this indenture made 5th day of March 1757 between John Bayne of the County of Westmoreland

and Parish of Washington of the one part and William Quesenbury, the elder of the aforesaid parish and county, planter of the other part. Whereas William Quesenbury was seized and possessed of a tract of land lying in the parish and County aforesaid containing 469 acres as tenant in fee tail and the said William Quesenbury being minded and willing to sell and dispose of the same did pursuant to the act of assembly in such cases made and provided sue out of the secretary's office of this colony his majesties writ the nature of an Ad Quod Damnun to the sheriff Westmoreland directed by virtue of which said writ the sheriff having cost inquisition to be made on the said lands of 12 good and indifferent men of his bailiwick and having returned that the said lands were under the value of £200 and that it was a separate parcel and not contiguous to other entailed land in the possession of the said William Quesenbury, the said William Quesenbury therefore for good and valuable consideration to him paid by an indenture of bargain and sale convey and make over to John Bayne the said tract of land and premises. The said John Bayne in consideration of the sum of 50 pounds current money of Virginia to sell unto the said William Quesenbury part of the above-mentioned tract of land lying and being on the north side of the main road where he now lives containing 250 acres.

In the presence of   John Bayne
Matthew Bayne
Nathaniel Butler
Joseph Eidsen
William Weaver (his mark)

Westmoreland Sct. At a Court held for the said County the 26th day of April 1757 this deed of land pass from John Bayne to William Quesenbury together with the receipt for the consideration thereon endorsed was presented into Court and proved by the oath of Nathaniel Butler, Joseph Eidsen and William Weaver witnesses thereto and on the motion of the said Quesenbury is admitted to record.
Recorded the 30th day of April 1757 George Lee CCW

Page 71.
Lee to Yeates Lease
This indenture made the 18th day of June 1756 between Henry Lee of the Parish of Dettingen in the County of Prince William, Esq. of the one part and Traverse Yeates of the Parish of Cople and the County of Westmoreland, taylor of the other part. Witnesseth that Henry Lee in consideration of the yearly rents and covenants herein after named has demised granted and to farm let unto Traverse Yeates all that massuage or tenant of land now in possession of the said Traverse Yeates line by Lane's mill and bounded by the land of Peter Lamkin and Rust which the said Henry Lee purchased of Richard Lee, Esq. containing 40 acres or more. To have and to hold the said parcel of land for and during the natural lives of the said Traverse Yeates yielding and paying yearly during the life of the said Yeates unto the said Henry Lee [missing] money of Virginia on the 27th day of November and each year. In witness whereof the parties to these presents have interchangeably set their hands and seals this day and year above written.

Sealed and delivered in the presence of us   Henry Lee
Joseph Lane   Traverse Yeates
James Woodson
John Tidwell
Francis Farrell
Henry Bryan

Westmoreland Sct. At a Court held for the said County the 26th day of April 1757 Henry Lee, Esq. and Traverse Yeates presented the within instrument of writing into court and acknowledged each to the other and on the motion of [missing] recorded the 30th [missing]   Test: George Lee CCW

Page 73.
Beard to Blair Indenture
Indenture made 18 April 1757 between John Beard, John Hilton and Ann Hilton of the Parish of Washington and County of Westmoreland of the one part and James Blair of the Parish and County aforesaid, merchant of the other part. Witnesseth that John Beard in consideration of 41 pounds

current money of Virginia paid by James Blair which the said John Beard, John Hilton and Anne Hilton acknowledge has sold unto James Blair all that tract of land lying in Washington Parish containing by estimation 107 acres and bounded as follows; vizt; beginning at a marked maple standing on the north side of Storke's Dam being a corner tree of the land of Meredith Edwards extending thence North 38 poles to a marked red oak, corner tree of Capt. Lawrence Washington's, thence North 72 ½° East 228 poles to a red oak corner tree of the said Washington's, thence South 74 poles to a marked white oak standing upon the said dam side and on the west side of a branch, thence up the meanders of the said dam to the beginning. In witness whereof the said John Beard, John Hilton and Ann Hilton have hereunto set their hands and seals this 10th day of April 1757

signed and sealed and delivered in presence of   John Beard
Andrew Monroe   John Hilton
Thomas Taylor   Ann Hilton (her mark)
William Rowe

Westmoreland Sct. At a Court held for the said County the 26th April 1757 this deed of land pass from John Beard, John Hilton and Ann Hilton his wife to James Blair together with livery and seizure thereon endorsed and the receipt thereon also endorsed signed, the said John Beard was proved in open court by the oaths, [Andrew Monroe], Thomas Taylor and William Rowe the witnesses [missing].
Recorded the 2nd day of May 1757   Test: George Lee CCW

Page 75.
Beard to Blair Privy Examination
To James Berryman, John Storke and John Monroe of the County of Westmoreland, greeting. Whereas John Beard of Washington Parish by his indenture bearing date 10th day of April as conveyed unto James Blair in fee estate 107 acres of land lying in said parish and county and whereas Ann the wife of John Hilton as dower in said land and cannot conveniently travel to our court to make acknowledgment of said convenience therefore we do give unto you or any two of you power to receive the acknowledgment. Witness George Lee, clerk of our said County Court the 18th day of April 1757.
Westmoreland. Pursuant to the within commission to us directed we have apart from her husband examined Ann Hilton wife of John Hilton touching her unconstrained consent and assent that the within named John Beard should pass deeds of feoffment to James Blair which he did freely. 10th day of April
John Storke
John Monroe
Westmoreland Sct. At a Court held for said County the 26th April 1757 the within commission was returned into court under the hand of John Storke and John Monroe that Ann Hilton the wife of John Hilton did freely relinquish her dower in the land sold by her son John Beard to James Blair therefore ordered to be recorded with said deed.
Recorded the 8th day of May 1757   Test: George Lee CCW

Page 77.
Butler's Will
In the name of God Amen, I Thomas Butler of the Parish of Washington and County of Westmoreland being sick and weak but of perfect sense and memory do make and ordain this my last will and testament.
Item I give and bequeath to my loving son James Butler the land given me by my father containing 66 acres more or less also the land I purchased of Col. Monroe containing 23 acres. Also, a Negro boy named Ben.
I give and bequeath to my loving son William Butler the land I purchased of William Moss to him and the heirs of his body lawfully begotten and for want of such heirs to my loving son John Butler and the heirs of his body lawfully begotten forever and first such heirs to the child my wife now goes with and if a son to him and his heirs forever.
Item my desire is that my loving wife shall [missing] all my personal estate during life [missing] so my desire is that my sons (to with) James, William, John and the child my wife goes with if a boy

Westmoreland County, Virginia Deeds & Wills DB13, 1756-1761

shall each and every of them have six years schooling and each of the girls two years schooling. I give and bequeath all my Negroes and personal state after my wife's decease to be equally divided between all my children except Negro Ben over and above the charge of all the rest to my son James Butler as above.
Item I make and ordain and appoint my beloved wife Isabel Butler and my friend George Monroe, Jr., executrix and executor or to this my last will and testament. In witness whereof I have hereunto set my hand and seal this 29th day of May 1756
Sealed and acknowledged in presence of   Thomas Butler
William Monroe, Sr.
Spence Monroe
Thomas Taylor
Westmoreland Sct. At a Court held for the said County on the 26 April 1757 this will was presented into Court by Isabel Butler one of the executors therein named who made oath thereto and being proved by the oath of William Monroe, Spence Monroe and Thomas Taylor three of the witnesses thereto it is ordered to be her recorded. And on the motion of the said Isabel and her performing what the law in such cases require certificate is granted for obtaining a probate thereof in due form.
Recorded the 12th day of May 1757   Test: George Lee CCW

Page 78.
Bayne to Quesenbury Lease
This indenture made in the 29th year of the reign of our Sovereign Lord George II King of Great Britain, France and Ireland King defender of the faith &c. between John Bayne of the County of Westmoreland and the Parish of Washington of the one part and William Quesenbury Sr. of the same parish and county of the other part. Witnesseth [1 shilling] sterling money to me in hand paid on or upon the last day of December yearly during his natural lives has leased to him all that parcel of land whereon he now lives containing 469 acres of land which bounds will appear by deed bearing date the 10th day of June 1756. Witness my hand and seal this 27th day of June 1756
Signed Sealed and delivered in the presence of us   John Bayne
William Bridges
Richard Bayne
Westmoreland Sct. At a Court held for said County 29 June 1756 John Bayne came into court and personally acknowledged this lease for lives passed by him to William Quesenbury to be his proper act and deed which on motion of the said Quesenbury was ordered to be recorded.
Recorded the 15th day of July 1756   Test: George Lee CCW

Page 78.
Quesenbury from Bayne Certificate
this is to certify that I have sold assigned and do agree to sell make over and confirmed to John Bayne the with and property of land as by the written lease for life the consideration for the same being fully paid and completed. As witness my hand and seal this fifth day of March 1757
Test   to William Quesenbury. Senior
Nathaniel Butler
Matthew Bayne
Joseph Eidsen
William [missing] (his mark)
Westmoreland Sct. At a Court held for the said County the 26th day of April 1757 the above certificate was proved in open court by the oath of Nathaniel Butler, Matthew Bayne and Joseph Eidsen and on motion of John Bayne ordered to be recorded.
Recorded this 12th day of May 1757   Test: George Lee CCW

Page 80.
Duncan to Simpson Indenture
This indenture made the 25th day of March 1757 between William Duncan in the Parish of Cople and the County of Westmoreland of the one part and Joseph Simpson of the Parish of Lunenburg and the County of Richmond of the other part. Witnesseth that William Duncan in consideration of

66 pounds 13 shillings and four pence lawful money of Virginia paid by Joseph Simpson has sold 100 acres of land I bought of Coleman Read near the branches of Nominy in the parish and County aforesaid being part of a patent of 400 acres of land first granted unto William Everett and George Brown dated the 22nd day of March 1665. In witness whereof the parties to these presents have interchangeably set their hands and asked their seals the day and year first above written.
Sealed and delivered in the presence of   William Duncan
George White
Daniel McKenny
Peter Lamkin
Westmoreland Sct. At a Court held for the said County 26 April 1757 William Duncan personally acknowledged this deed of your feoffment by him passed to Joseph Simpson, clerk together with the livery of seizure now endorsed to be his act and deed. And Ann Duncan the wife of the said William Duncan being first privately examined relinquished her right of dower all which on motion of the said Simpson is ordered to be recorded.
Recorded this 12th day of May 1757   Test: George Lee CCW

Page 82.
Sanford to Sanford Indenture
This indenture made this 30th day of May 1757 between Robert Sanford and Mary Parkington of the Parish of Cameron and County of Fairfax of the one part and Willoughby Sanford of the Parish of Washington and the County of Westmoreland of the other part. Witnesseth that Robert Sanford and Mary Parkington in consideration of 45 pounds current to them in hand paid by Willoughby Sanford has sold unto Willoughby Sanford all that tract of land lying in the Parish of Cople and County of Westmoreland containing 100 acres of land which [missing] by the last will and testament of his deceased [missing] third day of April [missing] here unto that will more fully appear and bounds as follows. vizt; beginning on the east side of a small [missing] joining to the land of Richard Moxley running thence N44° E94 poles to a poplar on the side of a branch thence on the lines Richard Moxley, Thomas Sanford, Daniel Moxley and Thomas Chilton to the beginning. In witness whereof the said parties to these presents have interchangeably set their hands and seals the day and year first above written.
Sealed and delivered in presence of us   Robert Sanford
John Washington   Mary Parkington (her mark)
Joseph Moxley
Thomas Washington
Thomas Sanford
William Sanford
Westmoreland Sct. At a Court held for the said County the 31st day of May 1757 this deed of feoffment together with the livery of seizen thereon endorsed for land passed from Robert Sanford and Mary Parkington to Willoughby Sanford was proved in open Court by the oath of John Washington, Joseph Moxley and Thomas Sanford witnesses thereto and upon motion of said Willoughby is admitted to record.
Recorded the ninth day of June 1757   George Lee CCW

Page 85.
Jackson's Will
Westmoreland Sct. At a court held for the said county the 31st day of May 1757 the last will and testament of Joseph Jackson, deceased was further proved by the oath of William Gilpin, a witness thereto.   Test: George Lee CCW

Page 85.
Tebbs to Lee Privy Examination
To Willoughby Newton, Richard Henry Lee, Richard Jackson and John Newton, greeting. Whereas William Tebbs and Mary Tebbs his wife of the County of Prince William and John Sorrell and Judith Sorrell his wife of the County of Westmoreland by their certain indenture of lease and release bearing date 13th November and the 1st day of December [missing] have conveyed unto Richard

Westmoreland County, Virginia Deeds & Wills DB13, 1756-1761

[Lee] [missing] of Westmoreland the fee simple estate of 116 or 117 acres of land being in Cople Parish and County of Westmoreland and whereas Mary and Judith cannot conveniently travel to our court to make acknowledgement do therefore command you to personally go to them and receive their acknowledgement. Witness George Lee, clerk of our said county court this 2nd day of December 1756.

Westmoreland Sct. By virtue of a commission to us directed bearing date 2nd day December 1756 to take the private examination of Mary Tebbs wife of William Tebbs of the county of Prince William and Judith Sorrell wife of John Sorrell of the County of Westmoreland touching their relinquishment of their rights of dower to 116 or 117 acres of land lying in the Parish of Cople and the County of Westmoreland as by a deed dated the 1st day of December 1756. We have privately examined the said wives apart from their husbands and they declared the same to be of their free will and consent and should be recorded. Given under our hand and seals this 24th day of May 1757.
Richard Jackson
John Newton

Westmoreland Sct. At a court continued and held for the said county the 1st day of June 1757 this commission for the private examination of Mary Tebbs and Judith Sorrell touching their passing inheritance and dower in a piece of land by them and their husbands and others sold to Richard Lee, Esqr. Was returned into court and it appearing that they were consenting, on motion of the said Lee admitted to record.
Recorded this 9th day of June 1757   Test: George Lee

Page 85.
Tebbs to Lee Lease
This indenture made the 13th day of November 1756 between William Tebbs of the county of Prince William [and Mary Tebbs his wife], Elizabeth McFarlane, widow of the County of Westmoreland, John Sorrell and Judith Sorrell his wife of Westmoreland and Ann Conway, widow of the county of Lancaster of one part and Richard Lee, Esq of the County of Westmoreland of the other part. Witnesseth that in consideration of five shillings the said William Tebbs and Mary Tebbs his wife, Elizabeth McFarlane, John Sorrell and Judith Sorrell his wife and Ann Conway have sold unto Richard Lee, Esq all that tract of land lying in Cople Parish and Westmoreland County containing by estimation 116 or 117 acres adjoining the land of Willoughby Allerton and running thence down to the Vinyard Branch thence along the meanders of the said branch and Crabb's Creek which premises formerly belonged to Henry Wiggington of the said county, deceased and afterwards descended to and became invested and the said William [Tebbs] as purchaser from Gerrard Davis and Elizabeth Miller by deed of lease and release dated the 26th and 27th days of March 1754 recorded, Mary, Judith and Ann as next heirs at law. To have and to hold from the day next before the day of the date herein during the full term of one whole year yielding and paying the rent of one ear of Indian corn before the last day of the last term to the intent and purpose that by virtue of these presents and of the statute for transferring uses into possession, he the said Richard Lee may be in the more full and actual possession of the premises. In witness whereof the said parties to these presents have interchangeably set their hands and seals the day and year first upon written.

Sealed and delivered in the presence of	
Daniel Tebbs	William Tebbs
Fleet Cox	Mary Tebbs
Elizabeth Cox	Elizabeth McFarlane
Joseph Lane	John Sorrell
	Judith Sorrell
	Ann Conway

Westmoreland Sct. At a court held for the said County the first day [of December 1756]. This lease of land passed from William Tebbs, Mary Tebbs, Elizabeth McFarlane, John Sorrell, Judith Sorrell and Ann Conway to Richard Lee, Esq. was proved by the oath of Joseph Lane and ordered to be lodged for further proof.

Westmoreland Sct. At a court held for the said County 28th day of June 1757. This lease of land passed from William Tebbs, Mary Tebbs, Elizabeth McFarlane, John Sorrell, Judith Sorrell and Ann Conway to Richard Lee, Esq. was further proved by the oaths of Daniel Tebbs and Fleet Cox

witnesses thereto and on motion of the said Lee admitted to record.
Recorded the second day of July 1757.   Test: George Lee CCW

Page 89.
Tebbs to Lee Indenture
This indenture made the first day of December 1756 between William Tebbs of the county of Prince William [and Mary his wife], Elizabeth McFarlane, widow of the County of Westmoreland, John Sorrell and Judith Sorrell his wife of Westmoreland and Ann Conway, widow of the county of Lancaster of one part and Richard Lee, Esq of the County of Westmoreland of the other part. Witnesseth that in consideration of 101 pounds current money, the said William Tebbs and Mary Tebbs his wife, Elizabeth McFarlane, John Sorrell and Judith Sorrell his wife and Ann Conway have sold unto Richard Lee, Esq all that tract of land lying in Cople Parish and Westmoreland County containing by estimation 116 or 117 acres adjoining the land of Willoughby Allerton and running thence down to the Vinyard Branch thence along the meanders of the said branch and Crabb's Creek which premises formerly belonged to Henry Wiggington of the said county, deceased and afterwards descended to and became invested and the said William [Tebbs] as purchaser from Gerrard Davis and Elizabeth Miller by deed of lease and release dated the 26th and 27th days of March 1754 recorded, Mary, Judith and Ann as next heirs at law
In witness whereof the said parties to these presents have interchangeably set their hands and seals the day and year first upon written.

Sealed and delivered in the presence of	William Tebbs
Daniel Tebbs	Mary Tebbs
Fleet Cox	Elizabeth McFarlane
Elizabeth Cox	John Sorrell
Joseph Lane	Judith Sorrell
	Ann Conway

Westmoreland Sct. At a court continued and held for the said County the first day of June 1757 this [indenture with] receipts thereon endorsed passed from William Tebbs, Mary Tebbs, Elizabeth McFarlane, John Sorrell, Judith Sorrell and Anne Conway to Richard Lee, Esq. was proved by the oath of Joseph Lane a witness thereto and ordered to be lodged for further proof.
Westmoreland Sct. At a Court held for the said County the 28th day of June 1757 this deed of release of land with the receipts thereon endorsed was further proved by the oath of Daniel Tebbs and Fleet Cox witnesses thereto and on the motion of Richard Lee, Esq. admitted to record.
Recorded the second day July 1757.   Test: George Lee CCW

Page 93.
Garner to Brown Lease
This indenture made this 16th day of June 1757 between Abraham Garner of the County of Westmoreland, planter of the one part and John Brown of the said County of the other part, planter. Witnesseth the said Abraham Garner in consideration of the rents and covenants and services hereafter mentioned as demised granted let and to farm let unto John Brown 80 acres of land lying in Ragged Point Neck on Potomack River, beginning at a locust [missing] standing in the West and by the South line of Hurd's patent and going from thence West and by South into the said woods to a marked white oak a corner tree, and thence South East by a straight line to a marked pine at the head of a branch issuing out of a pond and thence along the said branch and pond to the beach on Potomack River side and thence up the river bank to the beginning locust post. To have and to hold the said plantation land and premises unto him the said John Brown and Mary Brown his wife and Barbara Brown their daughter and the longest liver of them paying yearly and every year to the said Abraham Garner his heirs or assigns on the 25th day of December the full sum and quantity of 950 pounds of crop tobacco and cask, only the first year excepted which he is to have rent free in consideration thereon he is to build a dwelling house and a tobacco house. In witness whereof the said parties have interchangeably set their hands and seals the day and year above written.

Signed Sealed and delivered in the presence of us	Abraham Garner
John Norwood	John Brown
Manley Brown (his mark)	

John Stowers
Westmoreland Sct. At a court held for the said county the 28th day of June 1757 this lease of land from Abraham Garner to John Brown was proved by the oaths of John Norwood, Manley Brown and John Stowers and on the motion of the said Brown is admitted to record.
Recorded the [missing]   Test: George Lee CCW

Page 95.
Steptoe's Will
In the name of God Amen, I James Steptoe of the Parish of Cople and the County of Westmoreland being now in perfect health and strength of body and mind do declare this my last will and testament.
Item I order all my just debts to be paid.
Item I give and bequeath to my son George Steptoe and the heirs of his body lawfully begotten all my lands in Yeocomico Neck and Westmoreland County and for want of such issue to my son James Steptoe and his heirs forever
Item I give and bequeath to my son George Steptoe and the heirs forever my part of the mill at Yeocomico Church owned by Mr. Daniel Tebbs and myself.
Item I give and bequeath to my son George Steptoe and the heirs forever [missing] my stock in Westmoreland county.
Item I give and bequeath to my son James Steptoe and the heirs of his body lawfully begotten my land on Pohick Run in Fairfax County granted by patent bearing date the 25th day of July 1728 to Col. George Eskridge for 640 acres and conveyed to me by deeds of lease and release bearing date 27th February 1755 and all my lands in the said county of Fairfax conveyed to me by Thomas Winslow and Samuel Earle and my water mill and for want of such issue to my son Thomas Steptoe and his heirs forever.
Item I give and bequeath to my son Thomas Steptoe and his heirs forever 500 acres of land in Fairfax County granted by patent bearing dated the 6th day of November 1666 to Col. Nicholas Spencer and conveyed to me by Richard Lee, Esq. by deeds of lease and release bearing date the 26th and 27th days of February 1755.
Item I give and bequeath my stock of cattle, sheep and hogs and horses in the county of Fairfax to be equally divided between my two sons James Steptoe and Thomas Steptoe.
Item I give and bequeath my negroes to be equally divided between my children now living and [missing] child [missing] now [missing] with when my children arrives at [missing] years and those negroes given to my daughters when they marry if that should be before they arrive at the age of twenty-one as my executors think proper.
Item I give and bequeath to my daughter Ann Steptoe my silver tankard.
Item I lend to my wife Elizabeth Steptoe all my household furniture during her widowhood except the tankard given to my daughter Ann Steptoe and afterwards to be equally divided among my children.
Item I give my wife Elizabeth Steptoe one third part of my lands and negroes as her dower in my land and negroes
Item I give my wife Elizabeth Steptoe one third part of all my stocks and childs part of my personal estate besides what legacies I have left her.
Item I give my wife Elizabeth Steptoe my chariot and six horses that usually carry it.
Item I desire my estate may be kept together until my children arrives at their respective ages of twenty-one years for their maintenance and education and the profits to be then divided among them in the same manner as my negroes.
Item I give and bequeath the dower negroes given to my wife Elizabeth Steptoe to be divided among my children as my negroes before given.
Item I give and bequeath my household furniture after my wife's widowhood on death to be equally divided among my children.
Item my will and desire is that my son George Steptoe [schooling] be continued and educated in Britain at the expense of my estate and be brought up to some profession as my executors think proper.
Item I desire my two sons James Steptoe and Thomas Steptoe to be educated out of my estate

and to have as good as education as my estate will afford and to be brought up to some profession or calling as my executors think.
(Item my wife] Elizabeth Steptoe may have the bringing up of my daughter Ann Steptoe and my sister [Canell/Carrell ?] the bringing up of my daughter Elizabeth.
[mm note: His sister appears to be Mary the widow of Henry Asbury who married Patrick Connelly]
Item I revoke all former wills by me made and do constitute and appoint my wife Elizabeth executrix during her widowhood, my friends Richard Lee, Philip Ludwell Lee and George Lee of the County of Westmoreland, Esq. executors and guardians to my children.
In witness whereof I have set my hand and seal the 10th day of May 1755.
Signed Sealed published and declared in the presence of   James Steptoe
Nathaniel Jackson
Stewart Redman
Thomas Lawson
Westmoreland Sct. At a court held for the said county the 28th day of June 1757 this last will and testament was presented into court by Elizabeth Steptoe, Philip Ludwell Lee, George Lee and Richard Lee the executors therein named who made oath thereto and being proved by the oaths of Nathaniel Jackson, Stewart Redman and Thomas Lawson the witnesses thereto is [missing] or of the said executors and their performing what the law required in such cases certificate is granted them for obtaining a probate thereof in due form.
Recorded the 7th day of July 1757   Test: George Lee CCW

Page 98.
Omohundro to Omohundro Lease
This indenture made the 28th day of June 1757 between John Omohundro of Westmoreland County, planter of one part and John Omohundro, Jr., of the same county, planter of the other part. Witnesseth that John Omohundro in consideration of the rents reservations and covenants herein after mentioned has demised granted let and to farm let by these presents unto John Omohundro, Jr., that tract of land with the appurtenances lying in the Parish of Cople and the County of Westmoreland containing by estimation 80 acres of land and bounded as followeth. vizt; Beginning at the mouth of the Wolf Pit Swamp and running up the said swamp to a market forked white oak tree thence from the said swamp along a line to a marked chestnut tree thence up to the road, thence down the said road to a marked corner chestnut stump that divided the land of Richard Omohundro and William Sanders land thence along the said Omohundro's line to a corner red oak thence along a line between Philip Sanders and the said William Sanders to the first beginning. To have and to hold the said tract during the natural life of John Omohundro and John Omohundro, Jr. to pay yearly and every year to John Omohundro his heirs or assigns one ear of Indian corn which payment is to commence on the 30th day of June 1758. In witness whereof the parties to these presents have hereunto set their hands and seals the day and year first above written.
Signed Sealed and delivered in presence of   John Omohundro
William Taylor
William Omohundro
Thomas Chambers
Westmoreland Sct. At a court held for the said county the 26th day of July 1757 John Omohundro came into court and personally acknowledged his deed of lease of land to John Omohundro, Jr., which on his motion is admitted to record.
Recorded the 29th of July 1757   Test: George Lee CCW

Page 101.
Hutt & wife to Hutt Indenture
This indenture made the 21st day of July 1757 between Gerrard Hutt and Mary Hutt his wife of the Parish of Cople and Gerrard Hutt, Jr., of the aforesaid parish and county of the other part. Witnesseth that the said Gerrard Hutt and Mary Hutt his wife in consideration of one shilling paid by Gerrard Hutt, Jr., has sold by these presents two plantation tracts containing 310 acres. One tract that was formerly Joseph Hardwick's containing 140 acres and the other tract formerly Thomas Blundle's and those vested in William McKenne containing 170 acres lying in the Parish of Cople

and the County of Westmoreland. The first tract of land joining to Mr. Robert Carter & Mr. William Lane and the other tract that contains 170 acres joining to Thomas Robinson's land and Col. Ashton's land. In witness whereof the parties to these presents have hereunto set their hands and seals the day and year first above written.
Signed Sealed and delivered in presence of us
William Robinson (his mark)
James Robinson
Thomas Redman Robinson (his mark)
Westmoreland Sct. At a court held for the said county the 26th day of July 1757 Gerrard Hutt came into court and personally acknowledged this deed of feoffment together with livery and seizen thereon endorsed by him passed to his son Gerrard Hutt, Jr., to be his act and deed which on motion of the said Gerard was ordered to be recorded.
Recorded the 30th July 1757   Test: George Lee CCW

Page 104.
Naughty's will
In the name of God Amen, I James Naughty, Jr., of Westmoreland County being very sick and weak in body but of perfect sense and memory do make and declare this to be my last will and testament.
Item I give and bequeath to my father James Naughty two negroes named Tom and Dick during his natural life and after his death to my brother John Naughty and heirs of his body and for want of issue to my sister Mary Garrard and her heirs forever.
Item I give and bequeath to my sister Mary Garrard three negroes named Nell, Lett and Nell's boy with all their increase during her life and after her death to be equally divided between her two eldest children forever.
Item I give and bequeath to my brother all my goods and chattles but what is already disposed of he paying my debts which is justly due.
Lastly, I appoint William Garrard and John Naughty to be my executors of this my last will and testament. In witness whereof I have set my hand and seal this 12th day of April 1755.
In the presence of   James Naughty
Spence Monroe
William Price
John Higdon
Westmoreland Sct. At a court held for the said county the [missing] 1757 was presented into court by William Garrard and John Naughty the executor therein named who made oath thereto as the law directs and the same also proved by the oath of John Higdon one of the witnesses thereto is admitted to record and on the motion of the said executors and their performing what the law is such cases requires certificate is granted them for obtaining a probate thereof in due form.
Recorded the 30th of July 1757   Test: George Lee CCW

Page 105.
Washington & Wife to Blair Lease
This indenture made this 25th day of September 1757 between Henry Washington and Ann Washington his wife in the county of Middlesex of the one and James Blair of the County of Westmoreland on the other part. Witnesseth that the said Henry Washington and Ann Washington his wife in consideration of five shillings lawful money of Great Britain paid by James Blair has sold to him all the tract of land containing 140 acres lying on Roziers Creek in the Parish of Washington and County of Westmoreland beginning at the head of Roziers Creek and running down the creek the several meanders thereof to a spanish oak on the bank near the house where Job Sims formerly dwelleth, thence North 20° West to the road, thence West 3° South to the gate of the said Job Sims, thence South 42° to a water oak thence South 38° West along a line of marked trees to a white oak and a red oak, thence South 58° West to a small hickory, thence to a large white oak standing in the South West line of John Washington and along the same line to the beginning containing by estimate 140 acres. Being the same land exchanged by John Washington with Job Sims and now recovered by Henry Washington. To have and to hold the said land unto James Blair

from the 25th day of this instant September for and during the term of one whole year from thence next ensuing the date hereof fully to be completed and ended yielding and paying therefore one pepper corn on the feast of St. Michael the Arch Angel if demanded to the intent that by virtue of these presents and by force of the statute's for transferring uses into possession that the said James Blair his heirs and assigns may be in actual possession of all and singular the land and premises above mentioned. In witness whereof the said Henry Washington and Ann Washington his wife have hereunto interchangeably set their hands and seals this day and year first above written.

Signed sealed and delivered in the presence of us   Henry Washington
William Bernard   Ann Washington
John Bushrod
William Berryman

Westmoreland Sct. At a Court held for the said County the 27th day of September 1757 this lease of land passed by Henry Washington and Ann Washington his wife to James Blair was proved by the witnesses and on motion of the said Blair admitted to record.
Recorded the 30th day of September 1757   Test: George Lee CCW

Page 107.
Washington & Wife to Blair Indenture
This indenture made the 26th day of September 1757 between Henry Washington and Anne Washington his wife in the County of Middlesex of the one part and James Blair of the County of Westmoreland of the other part. Witnesseth the said Henry Washington and Ann Washington in consideration of 150 pounds current money of Virginia paid by James Blair has sold 140 acres of land be the same that the said James Blair being in actual possession whereof by virtue of a lease made thereof bearing date the day before the date of these presents and of the statute for transferring uses into possessions all that tract or parcel of land lying on and Parish of Washington and County of Westmoreland beginning at the head of Roziers Creek and running down the creek the several meanders thereof to a spanish oak on the bank near the house where Job Sims formerly dwelleth, thence North 20° West to the road, thence West 3° South to the gate of the said Job Sims, thence South 42° to a water oak thence South 38° West along a line of marked trees to a white oak and a red oak, thence South 58° West to a small hickory, thence to a large white oak standing in the South West line of John Washington and along the same line to the beginning containing by estimate 140 acres. Being the same land exchanged by John Washington with Job Sims and now recovered by Henry Washington.
In witness whereof the parties before mentioned have hereunto interchangeably set their hands and seals this day and year first above written.

Signed sealed and delivered in the presence of us   Henry Washington
William Bernard   Ann Washington
John Bushrod
William Berryman

Westmoreland Sct. At a Court held for the said County the 27th day of September 1757 this deed of release for land passed by Henry Washington and Ann Washington his wife with the receipt thereon endorsed to James Blair, Gent., was proved by the witnesses and on motion of the said Blair admitted to record.
Recorded the 30th day of September 1757   Test: George Lee CCW

Page 107.
Washington & wife to Blair Privy Examination
To John Bushrod, William Berryman and John Newton of the County of Westmoreland, Gent., greeting. We do hereby authorize you or any two of you sometime before next court to take the privy examination of Ann Washington the wife of Henry Washington apart from her husband touching her willingness to the passing of certain deeds of lease and release for conveyance her right of dower to 140 acres of land sold by her husband to James Blair, merchant in Washington Parish in the County aforesaid.
Witness George Lee, clerk of the said court the 10th day of September.

Westmoreland County, Virginia Deeds & Wills DB13, 1756-1761

Westmoreland Sct. This commission for the privy examination of Ann Washington wife of Henry Washington being returned and it appearing that the said and was thereto consenting is ordered to be recorded.
Recorded the 30th day of September 1757   Test: George Lee CCW

Page 112.
Garner to Rust Indenture
This indenture made the 27th day of August 1757 between John Gardner [Garner] of the Parish of Cople and County of Westmoreland of the one part and Samuel Rust of the same Parish and County of the other part. Witnesseth that John Gardner in consideration of 15 pounds current money paid by Samuel Rust has sold to the said Rust all those lands containing by estimation [missing] being part of a tract of land granted by patent to William Walker in 1662 lying in the Parish of Cople and County aforesaid and bounded by the lands of Samuel Rust and Bradley Garner South East 175 poles to a corner near Capt. Rust's Mill and from thence up the side of the mill pond 130 poles to a branch from thence up the said branch and valley that heads in William Coward's pasture and from the head of the valley northerly to the beginning. In witness whereof the party first to these presents have hereunto set his hand and seal this day and year first above written.
Sealed and Delivered in the presence of us   John Gardner [Garner]
Jeremiah Jeffries
James Courtney
John Courtney
Westmoreland Sct. At a Court held for the said County the 27th day of September 1757 John Gardner [Garner] personally acknowledged this deed of feoffment with the livery and seizin thereon endorsed for land by him passed to Samuel Rust to be his act and deed, which on motion of the said Rust ordered to be recorded.
Recorded this 30th day of September 1757   Test: George Lee CCW

Page 114.
Vaulx's Will
I Robert Vaulx being sick and weak but of disposing sense and memory do dispose of my estate in the following manner.
Imprimis, I give unto my friend John Elliott 400 acres of land in Prince [William] County during his natural life and after his decease to his two sons and their heirs forever. Which 400 acres of land here intended to be devised his part of a larger tract in the aforesaid County. The residue of the said lands together with another lying and being in the province of Maryland I devise to John Bushrod, Augustine Washington, Edward Ransdell and William Bernard and their heirs in trust to be sold for the payment of my debts but my will is that if Mr. McLain [Paul McClan/ McClain] who formerly lived with my mother should be liable to purchase the tract of land in Maryland, that my aforesaid trustees shall convey it to him in fee simple upon his paying to them £100.
Item I give to my daughters Milly Vaulx and Molly Vaulx my tract of land in Brereton Neck into the heirs of their bodies lawfully begotten equally to be divided.
Item I give to my daughters Caty Vaulx and Kenner Vaulx into the heirs of their bodies begotten all my land in Nominy, Machodoc Neck to be equally divided between them.
Item I give [missing] and child my wife [missing] bodies begotten by tract of land adjoining to the land of Col. Philip Ludwell Lee to be equally divided between them.
Item I give to my two daughters Betty Vaulx and Sally Vaulx into the heirs of their bodies begotten the tract of land I purchased of John Elliott to be equally divided between them.
Item I give to my daughter Caty Vaulx the tract of land whereon I formerly lived called the "Ruins" and to the heirs of her body begotten. Also, I give to her a tract of land which I purchased of Hugh French.
Item I give to my daughters Betty Vaulx and Sally Vaulx and the heirs of their bodies begotten a mill lying in being in Washington Parish.
Item I give and devise to the child my wife now goes with if a boy all the before mentioned tracts of and to him and the heirs of his body lawfully begotten forever and if my said son should die without

heirs then my will and desire is that my land shall descend and go to as before is directed.

Item I give to my friend John Elliott during his life the use of part of a tract of land which I purchased from him, vizt; from Horse Swamp along the line of Lawrence Washington's tract of land back into the woods as far as can tend with his own labors. I also give him the use of certain stocks sold to me by bill of sale during his life and afterwards to descend to his two sons forever. I also give to the two sons a Negro a piece to be delivered to them when they shall arrive to the age of 21 years; but as there is a contest upon the validity of Major John Elliott's will, if the said will should be established and if the said John Elliott or his heirs should recover any part of the said land, I purchased of him I do hereby revoke all the devise and request to the said John Elliott his sons.

Item I give to John Elliott during his life the use of a Negro fellow Harvey and after his death to return and be divided in the same manner as the residue of my Negroes is here before directed to be divided.

Item I give to my daughter Caty Vaulx Negro girl named Hannah.

Item I give to Brereton Kenner Negro Moll in Brereton Neck.

Item I give to my beloved wife during her widowhood all the Negroes mentioned in a certain marriage contract together with my waiting man Peter, Lettice, Rose and Whipster and my desire is if my said wife should marry again that all the Negroes devised to her should be equally divided amongst my children.

Item I devise the rest of my Negroes to be equally divided among my children and my desire is that my executors shall only add so many to the Negroes secured by marriage contract to the children of my present wife as shall make [missing] daughters equal in the whole.

Item [missing] my [missing] profit of my mill during her widowhood upon her paying one third part of the charges in repair.

Item I devise that my wife may work any part of the lands devised to her children with her Negroes until the children shall arrive to the age of 21 years or are married.

Item I devise to my wife after my debts are paid the guardianship of my children by her and their respective estates before devised to them.

Item I give to each of my daughters by my former wife a good feather bed and furniture, the rest of my household goods except a desk, scultore and chest of drawers which I devise to be sold for the payment of my debts, I give to my beloved wife forever.

Item I give to my wife the use of all my plate (except a punch ladle which I give to Augustine Washington) for her life and after her death to the child she now goes with, if a boy otherwise to be equally divided among all my children.

Item I give my beloved wife the stocks upon the plantation of Lawrence Washington during her life and after her death to her children by me, I desire the rest of my stocks may continue upon the respective plantations for the use of my wife and family till my children respectively come to their age or are married and then to be equally divided.

Item I give to my beloved wife 2000 pounds of tobacco per annum to be paid her by my executors out of the rents of my lands exclusive of the lands in the marriage settlement.

I give her also my chair and horses, a woman's saddle and a horse called Spanker.

Item I give to my daughter Betty Vaulx my horse called Jocky and a saddle

I give to Lawrence Washington his choice of my unbroken horses

I give to William Bernard my law books

I give to Thomas Shadrach the stocks he made over to me by bill of sale,

I give to my son-in-law Lawrence Washington a suit of mourning clothes.

I give to Thomas Hughes wife 500 pounds of tobacco for taking care of my children.

I remit to Edward Muse and John Muse their respective debts.

I desire James Russell may be discharged from my service. I remit also to him his debts.

I give James Russell, Sr. 500 pounds tobacco which I desire may be paid him out of a debt due from Thomas Davis which he has in his hands by virtue of a detinue made on the said Russell for rent.

I give to Edward Ransdell my gun.

I give to John Bushrod my sword.

I give to John Storke my cutter.

I give my friend Francis Williams one ram and 10 ewes.

Westmoreland County, Virginia Deeds & Wills DB13, 1756-1761

I desire [missing] blacksmith Dick may be discharged from my [missing] to make lease to [missing] reserve [missing] rents 950 pounds tobacco per annum.
I give to Washington Parish four thousand pounds tobacco after my debts paid to be paid 1000 pounds per annum
I devise my executors may provide a suitable tombstone and wall in the graveyard with a wall three brick thick.
I give a suit of black and a suit of blue close already made Brereton Kenner.
The rest of my wearing clothes I give to John Elliott
If any of my land should be recovered from any of the children to whom it is devised, my will is that the other children shall make up that lost to the losing child out of their estates.
I give to my friend Francis Williams liberty to be at 100 gallons of cider per annum for six years out of my orchards, Elliott's plantation and that my negroes assist him to be at it.
Item as I suspect a judgment will pass against John Elliott and myself for 100 pounds which I am sensible must be paid out of my estate my desire is that the tract of land for which that debt was contracted may be sold for the payment of my debts.
Item I devise the bricks now made in the "Ruins" together with the shells may be burned immediately and if the child my wife now goes with be a boy that my executors hereafter named rebuild the house out of the profits of my estate as soon as may be and if the child my wife goes with is a girl and she is inclined to rebuild the house and be at two thirds expense I desire my executors to pay the other one third; and to her heirs all the plank surveyed by my sawyers at Brereton Neck.
Item I desire my executors immediately to repair after the last manner, the house I now live and to add to it a shed 12' x 16' for the use of my wife and children.
Item I desire my daughter Elizabeth Vaulx remain with my dear wife till she arrives at the age of 18 or marriage.
I desire my good friend Mrs. Ann Washington to take my daughter Sarah Vaulx to live with till she arrives to the age of 18 or marriage.
I desire my good friend Mr. Ransdell to take my daughter Molly Vaulx until she arrives to the age of 18 or marriage.
I appoint John Bushrod, Augustine Washington, Edward Ransdell and William Bernard executors of my will aforesaid. In witness whereof I have hereunto set my hand and seal this fifth day of August 1754.

Signed sealed and published in the presence of us   R. Vaulx
Thomas Shaw
John Muse
Francis Williams
Lovell Harrison
This by way of codicil my will which I desire may be annexed.
It is my desire and wish that Sarah Pearce have my daughter Milly Vaulx.
I give to William Vigour, carpenter [missing] him his trade.
My will is in case Richard Pearce should be so aged that my executors shall be of the opinion that he cannot support himself that then and in that case he shall be well supported out of my estate.
I give William Goffland all his time due to me.
Item I give my daughter Caty Vaulx the purchase I made of Richard Steele of a certain stream and woodland ground for a water mill to her and her heirs forever.
Given under my hand and seal this 8th day of August 1754
Sealed and acknowledged in presence of   R. Vaulx
Francis Williams
B. Weeks
Thomas Hughes
Westmoreland Sct. At a court continued and held for the said County the 26th day of March 1755 this last will and testament of Robert Vaulx, deceased and his codicils was presented into Court by John Bushrod and Augustine Washington, Gent., two of the executors therein named who made oath thereto as the law directs that the will was proved by the oaths of John Muse and Francis Williams and the first codicil by Benjamin Weeks and Francis Williams. The said will and codicils

Page 41

ordered to be lodged for further proof and on motion of the said executors and their performing what the law in such case requires certificate is granted them for obtaining a probate thereof in due form.   Test: George Lee CCW

Westmoreland Sct. At a court held for the said County this 27th day of September 1757 the above will of Robert Vaulx, Gent., deceased being further proved by the oath of Lovell Harrison a witness thereto and the first codicil further proved by the oath of Thomas Hughes a witness to the last will and codicil, and ordered to be recorded

recorded the second day of October 1757   Test: George Lee CCW

Page 120.
Courtney & Wife to Tebbs Indenture
This Indenture made the 15th day of October 1757 between James Courtney and Margaret Courtney his wife of the Parish of Cople and the County of Westmoreland on the one part and Daniel Tebbs of the same parish and county of the other part. Witnesseth that the said James Courtney in consideration of 21 pounds 10 shillings current money has sold Daniel Tebbs his moiety or half part of a water grist mill standing on Tebbs Run and commonly called and known by the name of Courtney's Mill in the parish and county aforesaid, together with two acres of land to be laid off on each side and contiguous to the said mill. In witness whereof the parties above mentioned have hereunto set their hands and seals the day and year first mentioned.

Signed Sealed and delivered in presence of   James Courtney
Jeremiah Courtney   Margaret Courtney (her mark)
Daniel Tebbs, Jr.
Stephen Self (his mark)
Peter Mullins

Memorandum, October 1757 the within James Courtney and Margaret Courtney his wife made livery and seizen of the mill and two acres by turf and twigg and the ring of the door of the house on the land unto Daniel Tebbs.
In the presence of us
Jeremiah Courtney
Daniel Tebbs, Jr.
Stephen Self (his mark)
Peter Mullins
Ashton Lamkin

Westmoreland Sct. At a court held for the said court the 25th day of October 1757 this deed of feoffment passed from James Courtney and Margaret Courtney his wife together with livery and seizen and receipt for consideration thereon endorsed to Daniel Tebbs was proved in open court by the oaths of Daniel Tebbs, Jr., Jeremiah Courtney, Peter Mullins witnesses thereto and on the motion of the said Tebbs admitted to record.

Recorded the 27th day of October 1757   Test: George Lee CCW

Page 120.
Courtney & Wife to Tebbs Privy Examination
To Willoughby Newton, Samuel Oldham and Richard Jackson, Gent., greeting. Whereas James Courtney of the County of Westmoreland and Margaret Courtney his wife by indenture dated 15th October 1757 have conveyed unto Daniel Tebbs of the county aforesaid the fee simple estate of a water grist mill and two acres in the Parish of Cople and the said Margaret Courtney cannot conveniently travel to our court to make acknowledgement. Therefore, we do hereby authorize you or any two of you sometime before next court to take the privy examination of Margaret Courtney the wife of James Courtney apart from her husband touching her willingness to the passing of certain deeds of lease and release for conveyance her right of dower to a water grist mill and two acres sold by her husband to Daniel Tebbs in Cople Parish and the County aforesaid.

Witness George Lee, clerk of the said court the 22nd day of October.

Westmoreland Sct. At a court held for the said county the 25th day of October 1757, this commission for the privy examination of Margaret Courtney wife of James Courtney for the relinquishment of her rights of dower and inheritance being returned and it appearing that the said

and was thereto consenting is ordered to be recorded.
Recorded the 27th day of October 1757   Test: George Lee CCW

Page 124.
Black to Elphinston Mortgage
This Indenture made this 30th day of March 1757 between William Black of St. Mary's County, Maryland of one part and James Elphinston of Aberdeen in North Britain but present in Virginia of the other part. Witnesseth that William Black in consideration of 250 pounds current money has sold unto James Elphinston one messuage or tract of land known by the name of Pope's Quarter lying in Washington Parish and county of Washington containing 200 acres as also the Negro slaves thereon, vizt; Dick, Philaday, Emunidie, Venus and her child. Provided always that if the said William Black do well and truly pay unto the said James Elphinston on the 1st day of April ensuing the full and just sum of 250 pounds current money then this present indenture shall cease and be void. In witness whereof the said William Black hath hereunto set his hand and seal this day and year above written.
Signed Sealed and delivered in the presence of   William Black
Alexander Spark, Robert Mundie
M. Rose, William Templeman
Westmoreland Sct. At a court held for the said county the 27th day of September 1757 this mortgage passed from William Black to James Elphinston was proved by [missing] Alexander Spark, two of the witnesses [missing].
Westmoreland Sct. At a court held for the said county the 25th day of October 1757, this mortgage passed from William Black to James Elphinston and was further proved by the oath of William Templeman a witness thereto and ordered to be recorded.
Recorded the 30th day of October 1757   Test: George Lee

Page 126.
Higdon and Wife to Butler Indenture
This indenture made the 24th day of October 1757 between John Higdon and Sarah Higdon his wife of the Parish of Washington and County of Westmoreland of the one part and Lawrence Butler of the parish and county aforesaid, Gent., of the other part. Witnesseth that whereas James Mason was in his life time and at the time of his death seized and possessed of a tract of land lying upon Mattox Creek in the aforesaid parish and county in fee simple and being about to depart this life did give and devise the same to John Higdon by his last will and testament in writing and the said John Higdon so seized as tenant in fee tail after the death of James Mason being minded and willing to sell and dispose of the same did pursuant to the act of assembly in such cases made and provided sue out of the Secretary's office his majesties writ of Ad Quod Damnum to the sheriff of Westmoreland [missing] less value than 200 pounds sterling and it would not be to the damage of prejudice of those claiming in reversion or remainder by from or under the said John Higdon and that the same was a separate parcel and not contiguous to other entailed lands in the possession of John Higdon. The said John Higdondid sell and convey the said land to Matthew Bayne in fee simple. And whereas Matthew Bayne afterwards for a valuable consideration paid by John Higdon by and indenture of bargain and sale did reconvey to him in fee simple the whole tract of land except 66 acres for which Matthew Bayne had paid to John Higdon a valuable consideration upon his execution of the conveyance. Now this Indenture witnesseth that John Higdon in consideration of 126 pounds has sold unto Lawrence Butler the remaining part of said tract of land containing 124 acres and bounded as follows to wit; beginning at the mouth of Mary Underwood's gut dividing this land from the land of Lawrence Butler, thence up the gut to a small branch, thence up the branch to near the head thereon, thence South 40° West 92 poles to a corner post of this land and the land of the said Butler, thence North 64° West 46 poles to Matth[missing] East 26 poles to the head [missing] the said branch to the creek, thence down the creek to the beginning. In witness whereof the said John Higdon and Sarah Higdon have hereunto set their hands and seals the day and year first written.
Signed Sealed and Acknowledged in the presence of   John Higdon
Christopher Butler   Sarah Higdon (her mark)

John Brahan
John Shaw
Westmoreland Sct. At a court held for the said county the [x] day of November 1757 this deed was [missing] and Sarah his wife together with the receipt thereon endorsed to be their act and deed and the said Sarah Higdon being privily examined relinquished her dower which on motion by Lawrence Butler is admitted to record.
Recorded the 5th day of December 1757   Test: George Lee CCW

Page 129.
Bernard & Wife to Bernard Deed of Gift
This indenture made the 13th day of October 1757 between Richard Bernard and Elizabeth Bernard his wife of the Parish of St. Paul and the County of Stafford of the one part and William Bernard of the Parish of Washington and the County of Westmoreland, Attorney at Law of the other part. Witnesseth that the said Elizabeth Bernard in consideration of the natural love and affection which he hath and bear unto William Bernard, her son as for his better maintenance as given by these presents all that tract of land lying on the head of Upper Machodoc Creek in the Parish of Washington and County of Westmoreland containing by estimation 229 acres whereon William Hutcherson, Samuel Crange and Peter Crafford now lives. In witness whereof the said Richard Bernard and Elizabeth Bernard have hereunto set their hands and seals the day and year first above written.
Signed sealed and delivered in presence of   Richard Bernard
Andrew Monroe   Elizabeth Bernard
John Lovell
John Bulger
Westmoreland Sct. At a court held for the said County the 29th day of November 1757 this deed of gift passed from Richard Bernard and Elizabeth Bernard his wife to William Bernard was proved by the oath of Andrew Monroe, John Lovell and John Bulger witnesses to it and there upon ordered to be recorded.
Recorded the 6th day of December 1757   Test: George Lee CCW
(Page 130-132 Elizabeth Bernard Privy Examination commission recorded the 29th day of November 1757 and Release of Dower recorded 6th day of December 1757)

Page 132.
Duncan's Will
In the name of God Amen, I George Dunkin [Duncan] of the Parish of Cople and County of Westmoreland being sick and weak in body but of sound sense and memory do make and constitute this my last will and testament in manner and form following.
Item I give and bequeath unto my two sisters Elizabeth Dunkin and Sarah Dunkin all my estate both real and personal after my death is paid to be equally divided between them and their heirs forever and of either of these my two sisters should die without issue it is my desire that the other sister should be my whole and sole heir to all my estate.
Item I do hereby nominate and ordain my true and trusty friend Nathaniel Jackson, Jr., of the same Parish and County my full and sole executor of this my last will and testament. Whereof these presents set my hand and seal this 31st day of December 1757.
Signed sealed published and declared in the presence and hearing of us. George Dunkin
Charles McColley [McCauley], Thomas Taylor (his mark)
Westmoreland Sct. At a Court held for the said County the 28th day of February 1758 this last will and testament of George Dunkin, deceased was presented into Court by Nathaniel Jackson the executor therein named who made oath thereto as the Law directs and the same being also duly proved by the oath of Charles McColley and Thomas Taylor the witnesses thereto is admitted to record and on motion of the said executor in his performing what the law in such case requires certificate is granted him for obtaining a probate thereof in due form thereon.
Recorded the third day of March 1758   Test: George Lee CCW

Page 133.

Westmoreland County, Virginia Deeds & Wills DB13, 1756-1761

Suggett's Wife to Morton Privy Examination

To Thomas Slaughter, Nathaniel Pendleton and William Williams, Gent., greetings. Whereas James Suggett of the County of Culpeper by his indenture bearing date the 13th day of October 1756 did convey unto William Morton the County of Westmoreland in fee simple estate of 150 acres lying in the Parish of Cople and County of Westmoreland and whereas Jemima Suggett the wife of James Suggett to record make acknowledgment of the said conveyance. Therefore, we give you for any two of you are to receive the acknowledgment.
Witness George Lee clerk of our said County Court the 10th day of November
Westmoreland Sct. At a Court held for the said County the 28th day of March 1758 this commission for the privy examination of Jemima Suggett the wife of James Suggett whether relinquishment of her right of dower and inheritance to the lands her husband sold to William Morton being returned and she being thereto consenting ordered to be recorded.
Recorded the third day of April 1758   Test: George Lee CCW

Page 135.
Sanford to Sanford. Deed of Gift

I Thomas Sanford the County of Westmoreland for the entire love and affection to my son Youell Sanford have given unto him 65 acres of land which lies on the south side of the land called the Muster Field formerly belonging to my father and now called the Old Plantation land bounded on the lands of Joseph Stone, Foxhall Sturman and Richard Sanford which said land did formerly belonged to John Sturman the elder and was by him given to his daughter Dorcas Sanford and is now become the property of Thomas Sanford. Confirmation whereof I the said Thomas Sanford have set my hand and seal this [missing] five [missing] 1758
Signed Sealed and delivered in presence of us   Thomas Sanford
William Porter
John Luttrell
Westmoreland Sct. At a Court held for the said County the 28th day of March 1758 Thomas Sanford personally acknowledged his deed of gift of land to his son Youell Sanford; [at the same time] Margaret Sanford his wife being first privily examined relinquished her right of dower to the same which on motion of the said Youell Sanford ordered to be recorded
Recorded the third day of April 1758.   Test: George Lee CCW

Page 136.
Robinson's Will

In the name of God Amen, I Michael Robinson the County of Westmoreland being weak and sickly of body but of perfect sense and sound memory do make and ordain this to be my last will and testament in manner and form following.
Item I give and bequeath to my loving wife Frances Robinson all my whole estate of what kind soever to her my said loving wife and her heirs forever.
Item and [missing] I appoint and ordain my loving wife [missing] and Thomas Sanford [missing] of this my last will and testament. In confirmation whereof I have hereunto set my hand and affixed by seal this 7th day of December 1757.
Signed Sealed and delivered in the presence of us   Michael Robinson
Augustine Sanford
James Whitfield (his mark)
Westmoreland Sct. At a court held for the said county the 25th day of March 1758 this last will and testament of Michael Robinson, deceased was presented into court by Thomas Sanford his executor therein named who made oath thereto and being proved by the oath of James Whitfield a witness thereto (who also made oath that he saw Augustine Sanford subscribe it as a witness) was admitted to record. And on motion of the executor and his performing what the law in such cases requires, certificate is granted him for obtaining a probate thereof in due form.
Recorded 4th day of April 1758   Test: George Lee CCW

Page 137.
Mill's will

Westmoreland County, Virginia Deeds & Wills DB13, 1756-1761

In the name of God Amen, the 21st of October 1757, I William Mills of the County of Westmoreland being sick and weak in body but of sound and perfect memory do make this my last will and testament in manner and form as followeth.
Item I give and bequeath unto Esther Elliott, my housekeeper by two mares and all the linen made and unmade, all the cotton made and unmade, and all the woolen made and unmade, the crop of corn and the tobacco on the plantation that belongs to me. Also, the tobacco that Mdm. Ball owes me.
Item I give and bequest to William [missing] two sheep and a and a looking glass.
Item [I give and] bequest to Esther Elliott a chest along with the Pe[missing] estate I give to be equally divided [missing] William Bryant and John Bryant is to pay out of their parts all my just debts and funeral charges and all other debt that shall accrue.
I also constitute and appoint William Bowe executor of this my last will and testament.
Signed sealed and delivered in the presence of us   William Mills
William Degge
James Degge
Westmoreland Sct. At a Court held for the said County the 28th day of March 1758 this last will and testament of William Mills, deceased was presented into Court the executor therein named who made oath thereto as the Law directs in the same being also proved by the oath of William Degge and James Degge the witnesses thereto is admitted to record and on motion of the said executor and his performing what the law in such cases require certificate is granted him for obtaining a probate thereof in due form.
Recorded the 4th day of April 1758   Test: George Lee CCW

Page 138.
Harrison to Harrison Deed of Gift
I Samuel Harrison of the Parish of Cople and the County of Westmoreland for the natural love and affection and other good causes me thereunto moving have given unto my son William Harrison and his heirs forever 31 acres of land lying in the said parish and county being part of the tract I now live on and bounded as followeth. vizt; beginning at a walnut tree standing near the line between my[self] [missing] 83 ½ poles to a [missing] land from the land I bought of James Lane, thence along that line South 45° West 39 poles to the main road, thence along the main road North 55° West 30 poles to a red oak, thence North 5° East 40 poles to the beginning. In witness whereof I have interchangeably set my hand and affixed my seal this 24th day of March 1758.
Witness: Samuel Harrison
Samuel Harrison
Jeremiah Rust
Jeremiah Harrison
Westmoreland Sct. At a court held for the said county the 28th day of March 1758, Samuel Harrison came into court and personally acknowledged this deed of gift of land by him passed to his son William Harrison to be his proper act and deed which on motion of the said William was ordered to be recorded.
Recorded the 4th day of April 1758   George Lee CCW

Page 139.
Whiting's Will
In the name of God Amen, I Thomas Whiting of the Parish of Washington and County of Westmoreland being sick of body but of perfect sense … do make this my last will and testament.
I give and bequeath to my daughter Molly Whiting 4 pounds six shillings current money of Virginia.
I give and bequeath to my daughters namely Sally Whiting, Molly Whiting, Nelly Whiting and Lizey Whiting all my estate real and personal to be equally divided amongst them except to my daughter Molly Whiting or pounds six shillings over and above an equal share with the others as aforesaid.
My desire is that my land shall remain unsold and to my daughter Lizey is married or live to the age of 18 years during which time to be tenanted out to the greatest advantage for my children but if either of my daughters should marry before my daughter Lizey arise at the age of 18 my desire is that such daughter shall live on the land and pay to the others in moderate rent for the use of it till

my daughter Lizey is married or arrives at the age of 18 at which time I desire my land may be sold and the money arising thence be equally divided amongst my four children as above mentioned.
My desire is that my personal estate to be sold at two years credit.
My will is that my daughter Lizey Whiting shall be put to [?] years school the charges of which to be paid out of the rents of my land before division is made among my children.
My desire is that my daughter Molly Whiting liveth under the care and authority of Mary Dishman wife of Samuel Dishman and my daughter Lizey Whiting with and under the care of Elizabeth Monroe wife of Spence Monroe; and my daughter Nelly [missing] care of Henry Roe to be brought [missing].
My friends William Bernard, James Bankhead, John Monroe and Andrew Monroe, Jr., to be executors of this my last will and testament. In witness whereof I have hereunto set my hand and seal this sixth day of December 1757.
Signed sealed and acknowledged in the presence of   Thomas Whiting (his mark)
Thomas Butler
George Finch
Ann Finch (her mark)
Westmoreland Sct. At a court held for the said county the 28th day of March 1758
The last will and testament of Thomas Whiting, deceased was presented into court by Andrew Monroe, Jr. the executor therein named who made oath thereto as the law directs and the same being also proved by the oaths of George Finch and Ann Finch the witnesses thereto is admitted to record, and on motion of the said executor and his performing what the law in such cases requires certificate is granted him for obtaining a probate thereof in due form.
Recorded 5th day of April 1758   Test: George Lee CCW

Page 141.
Haborn vs Moore Processioner's Report
Westmoreland Sct. At a court held for the said county the 30th March 1756, George Lee, Gent., one of the churchwardens of Cople Parish presented into court a processioner's return under the hands of Francis Wright and Daniel Harrison certifying that they were stopped by Eleanor Heaborn [Haborn] from processioning the line between her and William Moore in presence of John Fleming, John Coombs and James [missing]. Whereupon pursuant to the act of assembly in that case provided it is considered by the court that the surveyor of the said County in company with an able jury of freeholders of the vicinage who are no ways concerned in interest or related by affinity or consanguinity to either of the parties, non-liable to any other just exceptions, to be summoned by the sheriff and sworn before Justice of Peace for the said County, to go upon the lands in difference between the said Eleanor Haborn and William Moore on the 14th day of April next, and lay off the bounds in dispute; the sheriff to attend the survey and remove force if any offered and the surveyor to return with a copy of said survey. Copy Test   George Lee CCW

Page 141.
Haborn vs Moore Plat & Survey
[Surveyors plat at bottom of page]
Westmoreland to Wit: Eleanor Heaborn [Haborn] vs William More [Moore] In obedience to and order dated the 10th day of March 1756 in a stop of processioning [missing] William Moore. The subscriber [in company of a jury sworn according to law] [missing] John Netherton, Gent., and the sheriff of the said County; met on the lands in difference in the Parish of Cople on the day mentioned in the said order first request of the plaintiff begun at where formerly stood and old stump proved by James Bailey to the plaintiffs beginning thence South 36° East 85 poles to a white oak corner at the letter "B" South 52° West 98 poles to a stake at the letter "C" then by the request of the jury began at the letter "A" his before and run the several courses as appears on the plot so as to include 60 acres of land which is laid down by the black dotted lines in the letters "A", "B", "C", "D", "P", & "N". Surveyed B. Weeks, S. W. Cty

Page 142.
Haborn vs Moore Jury Verdict

Westmoreland County, Virginia Deeds & Wills DB13, 1756-1761

Westmoreland Wit:
We the subscribers being duly sworn before Capt. John Newton, Gent., one of his majesties Justices for the said County pursuant to an order of the said County Court dated the 30th day of March 1756 met upon the lands in controversy between Eleanor Haborn, plaintiff, and William Moore defendant. We of the jury find for the plaintiff 60 acres of land according to the will of Thomas Moore the elder which courses and distances we refer to the survey plot. Given under our hands and seals this 15th day of April 1756.

Jeremiah Middleton	Benjamin Middleton, foreman
William Lane	John Critcher
John Bailey	John Brown
William Middleton	Michael Gilbert
John Fleming	Samuel Harrison
Samuel Smith	John Harrison

Westmoreland Sct. At a court continued and held for the said County the 30th day of March 1758 the surveyor's plan, support injuries verdict hereunto annexed in a stop of processioning made by Eleanor Heabornagainst William Moore returned into court pursuant to an act of the general assembly in order to be recorded.
Recorded fifth [missing] George Lee CCW

Page 143.
Ransdell's Will
In the name of God Amen, I Wharton Ransdell of Cople Parish and the County of Westmoreland being in perfect health do make this my last will and testament.

Item I give and bequeath unto my son Edward Ransdell the land whereon I now live to him his heirs and assigns also a piece of land I purchased of William Buckley adjoining to his land in the same manner, also my mulatto girl Susanna and my Negro girl baptized by the name Mary. Also, my silver watch and my silver hilted sword, also my still and worm and all my little casks.

Item there is a piece of land I purchased of Willoughby Newton on Beaver Dam Run of Aquia Creek in Stafford County, part of which I gave my daughter Sarah Elliott Peirce by deed of gift at the North West end of said land. And the residue I give to my son Edward Ransdell in the same deed and there being no division lined between them.

I do de[missing ...] design in those deeds [missing] to my said daughter [missing] end lines as they were made by Elias Davis' survey.

Item I give and bequeath unto my son Wharton Ransdell my Negro man George, and all my wearing close of every kind and nature

Item I give and bequeath unto my son William Ransdell a piece of land near the North Cobbler Mountain in Prince William County to him and his heirs and assigns forever. Also, my Negro girl Peggy and my mulatto boy Robin Wood

Item I given to my daughter Sarah Elliott Peirce 20 shillings to buy her a ring having already settled portion of her.

Item I given to my wife Sarah Ransdell my chair and chair harness and my horse colt Finch; my little horse called Draggon; my curtains and vallons that stands in the new closet and 6 cane chairs.

Item I give all the remainder of my estate to be equally divided between my wife Sarah Ransdell and my three sons, Edward Ransdell, Wharton Ransdell and William Ransdell.

Lastly, I nominate and appoint my wife Sarah Ransdell and my three sons Edward Ransdell, Wharton Ransdell and William Ransdell my whole and sole executors of this my last will and testament. In witness whereof I have but my hand and affixed my seal this 10th day of June 1755.

Sealed and declared in the presence of   Wharton Ransdell
Richard Parker, Thomas Sanford
William Bruer

Westmoreland Sct. At a court held for the said County the 25th day of April 1758 this last will and testament of Wharton Ransdell deceased was presented into Court by Edward Ransdell one of the executors therein named who made oath thereto as the Law directs and the same being also duly proved by the oath of Richard Parker, Thomas Sanford and William Bruer witnesses thereto is admitted to record, and on motion of the said executor and his performing what the law in such

cases requires certificate is granted him for obtaining a probate thereof in due form.
Recorded the [missing] George Lee CCW

Page 144.
Haikes & Wife to Ashton Indenture
This indenture made the 21st day of April 1758 between Richard Haikes and Mary Haikes his wife of the Parish of Washington and County of Westmoreland of the one part and Burditt Ashton of the said parish and county aforesaid of the other part. Witnesseth that Richard Haikes and Mary Haikes his wife in consideration of 21 pounds current money have sold to Burditt Ashton a tract of land lying in the parish and county aforesaid on Machodoc Creek on the North and South sides of a gut or cove called Hudson's Cove containing 50 acres and bounded to wit: beginning at a placed called Hudson's Landing running thence South West dividing the land from the lands belonging to and in possession of Margaret Settles, to a branch or run thence up the said branch till it forks and divides and from thence to the line of the land now in possession of Burditt Ashton and along the said line to Charles Ashton's line, thence to the creek and thence up the creek to the beginning. Which said lands conveyed are the southern dividend of a part of a tract of land escheated by and confirmed to Joshua Hudson by patent from the Proprietors office of the Northern Neck bearing date the 10th day of January 1704 for 100 acres., part thereof, to wit, 50 acres contained in a patent granted to Robert Howson and the residue thereof, the premises hereby sold and conveyed, contained in one other patent referenced being thereto [missing] appear. And whereas after the death of the said Joshua Hudson the 100 acres descended to Margaret Fry and from her to Margaret Settles and Mary Haikes as sisters and coparceners by the said Margaret Settles and Mary Haikes then the widow of John Welch now Mary Haikes amicably divided according to the above courses as by an indenture reciting the said courses of record in the county court of Westmoreland. In witness whereof the said Richard Haikes and Mary Haikes his wife have hereunto set their hands and seals the day and year written.
Signed Sealed & delivered in the presence of Richard Haikes (his mark)
James Blair Mary Haikes (her mark)
William Berryman
James Brown (his mark)
Westmoreland Sct. At a court held for the said county the 25th day of April 1758 this deed together with the livery of seizen and receipts thereon endorsed passed from Richard Haikes and Mary Haikes his wife to Burditt Ashton were all proved by the oaths of James Blair, William Berryman and James Brown witnesses thereto and the commission for the privy examination of Mary Haikes touching the relinquishment of her dower and inheritance to the said land being returned that she was thereto consenting are on motion of the said Burditt ordered to be recorded.
Recorded the 27th April 1758 Test: George Lee CCW

Page 148.
Harrison to Harrison Deed of Lease
We Samuel Harrison and Daniel Harrison of the Parish of Cople and County of Westmoreland of our own free will natural love and affection and for other good and sufficient causes as thereunto moving have given unto our brother Joshua Harrison for and during the term and space of his natural life 32 acres of land lying in the said parish and county aforesaid being part of the tracts of land we now live on and bounded as follows, vizt; beginning at a chestnut stump in the line of Samuel Harrison thence along his line South 50° East 169 poles to the land of James Self thence North 18° West 80 poles to a cedar standing in the old field thence North 40° West 36 poles to a cherry tree standing near the tobacco house thence North 92° West 84 poles to the beginning. In witness whereof we have hereunto set our hands and affixed our seals this 30th day of March 1758.
Signed Sealed and delivered in presence of Samuel Harrison
Samuel Harrison Daniel Harrison
John Harrison Sr.
John Harrison
Jeremiah Harrison
Westmoreland Sct. At a court held for the said county the [x] day of April 1758 Samuel Harrison

and Daniel Harrison came into court and personally acknowledged this deed of lease of land for life together with the livery of seizen thereon endorsed by them passed to their brother Joshua Harrison to be their proper act and deed and on motion of Joshua ordered to be recorded.
Recorded the 29th day of April 1758   Test: George Lee

Page 150.
Newton to Caddeen Lease
This indenture made the 2nd day of March 1758 between Willoughby Newton, Gent., of the Parish of Cople and the County of Westmoreland of the one part and Richard Caddeen, taylor of the parish and county of the other part. Witnesseth that the said Willoughby Newton in consideration of the yearly rents and covenants herein after reserved and contained to be done and performed hath demised, leased let and to farm let unto Richard Caddeen all that plantation of land whereon John Williams now lives which the said Willoughby Newton leased to Francis Self as by indenture of lease bearing date the 23rd day of September 1740 during the natural life of Francis Self or Catherine Self his wife or the longest liver; and the said Francis Self and Catherine Self his wife by assignment of the lease bearing date the 19th day of September 1753 made over the land [missing] to Matthew [missing….] to come and the said Matthew Trussell being now lunatic and therefore not capable of taking care of the said plantation and his wife having eloped from him so that there was no one left to comply with the articles and agreements on the behalf of the said Francis Self and Catherine Self his wife wherefore the lease became forfeited and Willoughby Newton reentered and took possession of the plantation which is bounded as follows; beginning at a forked poplar on Tuckers Run, corner to Garner extending thence along the said Garner's line NW to the road that from Nomini to Yeocomico Church, thence down the road to the going over place of the said run next to Netherton's plantation where the road that leads from poplar knoll to Yeocomico Church across the said Tuckers Run thence up the said run to the beginning containing 100 acres. To have and to hold the demised land and premises with all and other the appurtenances for this 1st day of January next ensuing for and during the term of the natural life of him the said Richard Caddeen and Hannah Caddeen his wife and John Caddeen their son and the life of the longest livery of them yielding and paying yearly and every year the annual rent of 630 pounds of net tobacco as the law shall direct tobacco payments on the 25th day of December and every year.
In witness whereof the parties to these presents hereunto interchangeably set their hands and seals the day and year first to this indenture writtten.
Signed Sealed and delivered in the presence of us   Willoughby Newton
George Lee   Richard Caddeen (his mark)
William Jett
Thomas Lawson
Westmoreland Sct. At a court held for the said county the 30th day of May 1758 Willoughby Newton, Gent., came into court and personally acknowledged this lease for lives by him passed to Richard Caddeen to be his proper act and deed which on motion of the said Caddeen was ordered to be recorded.
Recorded the 1st day of June 1758   Test: George Lee CCW

Page 152.
Strother to Dishman Bond
Know all men by these presents that I Sarah Strother of Washington Parish and the County of Westmoreland and held and firmly bound to James Dishman the same County in the penal sum of 110 pounds current money of Virginia for which payment well and truly to be made unto the said James Dishman his heirs and assigns. Sealed with my seal and dated the 29th day of May 1758. The condition of the above obligation is such that if the above [missing] Strother do relinquish all her dower rights in a tract [missing] 2 acres or thereabouts which James Dishman purchased of George Weedon by deed bearing date the ninth day of October 1757 then the above obligation to be void and of non-effect otherwise to remain in full force power and virtue.
Sealed and delivered in presence of   Sarah Strother (mark)
James Blair
Original Wroe

Westmoreland County, Virginia Deeds & Wills DB13, 1756-1761

Thomas Taylor
Westmoreland Sct. At a court held for the said County the 30th day of May 1758 this bond passed from Sarah Strother to James Dishman was proved with James Blair, Original Wroe and Thomas Taylor witnesses thereto and on motion of the said Strother was admitted to be record.
Recorded the fifth day of June 1758   Test: George Lee CCW

Page 153.
Rice's Will
In the name of God Amen, I Zorabable Rise of the Parish of Cople and the County of Westmoreland being at this time of sound mind although weak in body do make my last will and testament as follows.
I bequeath my eldest son Zorabable Rise one Negro man named Peter also a mulatto boy named William Potter, also a horse and a gun.
To my second son Simon Rise one bed.
Item I bequeath to my youngest son John Rise one mullato girl named Anne Potter.
Item I bequeath to my youngest Mary Rise one mulatto girl named Winifred Potter.
The rest of my personal estate to be equally divided between my wife Isabella Rise and all my children and it is my will and desire that no division shall be made in four years from this time in which space of time the debts is to be paid and I appoint my son Zorabable Rise and John Rise my executors. In witness whereof I have set my hand and seal this 19th day of May 1750.
Witness   Zorabable Rise (his mark)
Thomas Lambeth
Simon Rise
Westmoreland Sct. At a court held for said County the 30th day of May 1758 this last will and testament of Zorabable Rise, deceased was presented into Court by Zorabable Rise his son one of the executors therein named who made oath thereto as the law directs and the same being also proved by the oath of Thomas Lambeth & Simon Rise witnesses thereto is admitted to record and on motion of the said executor and his performing what the law in such cases requires certificate is granted him for obtaining a probate thereof in due form.
Recorded the first day of June 1758   Test: George Lee CCW

Page 154.
Smith & Wife to Moore Indenture
This Indenture made this 3rd day of November [missing] between Peter Smith and Eleanor Smith his wife of the Parish of Cople and County of Westmoreland, planter of one part and Robert Moore of the aforesaid Parish and county of the other part. Witnesseth that Peter Smith and Eleanor Smith his wife in consideration of 20 pounds current money has sold to Robert Moore all that plantation containing 41 acres situated in the Parish of Cople and County of Westmoreland being part of a tract of land Nicholas Smith formerly lived and now vested in Peter Smith and Eleanor Smith his wife and adjoining the land of John Bailey's deceased. In witness whereof the parties first above mentioned have hereunto set their hands and seals the day and year first mentioned.
Signed Sealed & delivered in presence of us   Peter Smith (his mark)
Gerard Hutt   Eleanor Smith (her mark)
Stephen Smith
Samuel Smith
[Note: On the 6th of November 1756 the within named Peter Smith and Eleanor Smith his wife delivered peaceably actual and quiet possession and seizen of the within granted land unto the within named Robert Moore according to the true form & effect of the within deed.]
Westmoreland Sct. At a court for the said county the 28th day of June 1757 this deed of feoffment with the livery and seizen endorsed passed from Peter Smith and Eleanor Smith his wife to Robert Moore was proved and Gerard Hutt and Samuel Smith two of the witnesses thereto and ordered to be lodged for further proof. Test: George Lee CCW
Westmoreland Sct. At a court held for the said county the [blank] day of May 1758, [missing] the livery and seizen endorsed passed from Peter Smith and Eleanor Smith his wife to Robert Moore was fully proved by the oath of Stephen Smith a witness thereto and thereupon ordered to be

recorded
Recorded the 2nd day of June 1758   Test: George Lee CCW

Page 156.
Davis' Will
I Hugh Davis of Westmoreland County, planter do make and appoint this my last will and testament in manner and form following;
My body to be buried at my plantation in the forest and my funeral at the discretion of my executor.
I give and bequeath my land to my son Peter Davis and his heirs forever.
I give and bequeath all the rest of my estate to be equally divided between my two children Peter Davis and Anne Bayley Davis.
I give and bequeath to my wife Elizabeth Davis what the law gives her.
I order my Negro Harry which I bought of John Middleton to be sold if my executor thinks proper.
Lastly, I appoint my two friends Richard Lee, Esq. and Mr. Fleet Cox executor of this my last will and testament and guardians to my children. In witness whereof I hereunto set my hand and seal the 9th day of December 1756.
Signed Sealed published in the presence of   Hugh Davis
Robert Middleton
[John Williams]
Westmoreland Sct. At a court held for the said county the 26th day of July 1757 the last will and testament of Hugh Davis, deceased was presented into court by Richard Lee, Esq. one of his executors therein named and being proved only by the oath of Robert Middleton one of the witnesses thereto is lodged for further proof.   Test: George Lee CCW
Westmoreland Sct. At a court held for the said county the 30th day of May 1758 the last will and testament of Hugh Davis, deceased was presented into court and fully proved by the oath of John Williams. Richard Lee, Esq. one of the executors therein named made oath thereto and his performing what the law in that case requires certificate is granted him for obtaining a probate thereof in due form.
Recorded the 2nd day of Jun 1758   Test: George Lee CCW

Page 157.
Callis Will
In the name of God Amen, I William Callis of Cople Parish in the County Westmoreland being sick of body but of perfect sense and memory do make and ordain this my last will and testament in manner following.
Item it is my will and desire all my just debts be paid.
Item it is my will and desire my executors sell my land in Machodoc Neck and the money arising therefrom to be applied to the payment of my debts.
Item I give all my Negroes to be divided by two sons Garland Callis and William Overton Callis.
Item I give and bequeath all my personal estate of what nature or kind soever be equally divided between my aforesaid sons Garland Callis and William Overton Callis.
Item I give unto my loving wife Mary Callis her riding horse and saddle over and above her lawful dower.
Item I give and bequeath the dower slaves after the death of my wife to be equally divided between my aforesaid two sons.
Lastly, I constitute and appoint my loving wife Mary Callis and my friends Col. George Lee and Col. Richard Lee executors of this my last will. In witness whereof I have hereunto set my hand and affixed my seal this 20th day of January 1758
Signed Sealed published before
Francis Callis, Francis Atwell
Richard Callis
Westmoreland Sct. At a court held for the said County the 30th day of May 7 58 the last will and testament William Callis deceased was presented into Court by Richard Lee one of the executors therein named and was proved by the oath of Francis Callis one of the witnesses thereto and ordered to be lodged for further proof. Test: George Lee CCW

Westmoreland County, Virginia Deeds & Wills DB13, 1756-1761

Westmoreland Sct. At a court held for the said County the 24th day of June 1758 last will and Testament of William Callis, deceased was further proved by the oath of Francis Atwell the witness thereto and was ordered to be recorded. Richard Lee, Esq. one the executors therein named made oath thereto and his performing all such things as salon this case is required certificate is granted him for obtaining a probate thereof.
Recorded 28 June 1758 Test: George Lee CCW

Page 159.
Blair to Wilkerson Lease
This indenture made the 27th day of May 1758 between James Blair, Gent., of Washington Parish in the County of Westmoreland of the one part and James Wilkerson of the same county and parish, planter of the other part. Witnesseth that James Blair in consideration of the annual rent of 950 pounds of crop tobacco in one caske has let to farm let all that tenement of land lying in the aforesaid County and bounded as followeth; beginning at a marked maple standing on the north side of the main branch of Mattox Creek and near the land Anthony Edwards extending thence northerly to the land John Wilkerson, thence easterly along the said John Wilkerson's land in James Whitfield's land to the said Blair's corner tree, thence southerly the main branch of Mattox Creek, then up the said main branch of Mattox Creek or near the same to the first beginning tree. It being a tract of land which James Blair lastly purchased of John Beard containing by estimation 107 acres. To have and to hold the said 107 acres of land unto the said James Wilkerson and his wife Mary Wilkerson and his son from the day of the date hereof for and during their lives yielding and paying to James Blair the aforesaid annual rent yearly upon demand after the 25th day of December yearly. In witness whereof the parties aforesaid have interchangeably set their hands and seals the day month and year first above written.
Signed sealed and delivered in presence James Blair
Andrew Monroe James Wilkerson
Original Wroe
Thomas Taylor

Westmoreland Sct. Held for the said County the 27th day of June 1758 James Blair, Gent., came into court and personally acknowledged this lease for lives of land by him passed to James Wilkerson to be his proper act and deed who on motion of the said Wilkerson ordered to be recorded.
Recorded the 28th day of June 1758 Test: George Lee

Page 161.
Lang to Newton Bill of Sale
Know all men by these presents that I Robert Lang of the Parish of Cople and the County of Westmoreland have this day bargained and sold unto Willoughby Newton the following goods, vizt;; two feather beds and furniture, six chairs, three iron pots and hooks, one frying pan, one chest and a trunk, also one sorrel mare, one gray mare and one mare colt, one whole bay horse, three cows, one steer and a bull yearling, 18 head of hogs and shoats, two pewter dishes, one Bason, five plates, one iron saddle, 12 case bottles, one spinning wheel and three stone jugs, all which I have this day delivered him in consideration of 26 pounds 8 shillings and 4 pence current money of Virginia which I owe to the said [missing] rents and other goods I had of him [missing] knowledge myself to be fully satisfied and paid for the above mentioned goods and stock now delivered to the said Willoughby Newton and I do by these presents warrant the same to him and his heirs and assigns from all claims. In witness whereof I have hereunto set my hand and seal this 22nd day of June 1758.
Signed sealed and delivered in presence of us Robert Lang
Westmoreland Sct. At a court held for the said County the 25th day of July 1758 Robert Lang came into court and personally acknowledged this bill of sale by him passed to Willoughby Newton together with the receipt thereon endorsed to be his proper act and deed and on motion of said Newton was ordered to be recorded.
Recorded the 26th day of July 1758 Test: George Lee CCW

Page 162.
Steptoe vs Allerton Land Divison
Westmoreland Sct. At a Court held for the said County the 27 day of June 1758
Willoughby Allerton and Ann Allerton   Htr ucfmfsy%%
by the said Willoughby her guardian   Chancery
Against Elizabeth Steptoe an infant by George Lee   Respondent }
her guardian
This day came the parties by their attorneys and by their mutual consent it is ordered that Richard Jackson, Daniel Tebbs and John Crabb do divide the land formerly held by Col. James Steptoe in Yeocomico Neck containing 220 acres with the appurtenances between the said complaint thence and the said respondents having due regard to quantity and quality and they also settle an account of the profits of the said land from the death of the said James Steptoe and allot unto the parties of each their proportionable part and report their proceedings therein under their hands in writing to the next court to be held for the County in order for a final decree. Copy Test: George Lee CCW
Westmoreland Sct. In obedience to an order of the said court in Chancery dated the 27th day of June 1758 we the subscribers being appointed in the order to divide the land formerly held by James Steptoe, Gent., deceased in Yeocomico Neck between Willoughby Allerton and Ann Allerton his wife, complainant and Elizabeth Steptoe an infant have divided the same as it will appear by the surveyor's plat hereunto annexed and likewise according to the said order say that the profits of the said land is to be of the value of 15 pounds current money per year from the death of the said James Steptoe, Gent.,
Given under our hands [missing]
Richard Jackson, [John Crabb, Daniel Tebbs]
[Surveyors Plat top of page 164]
Westmoreland July 5, 1758
Then surveyed for Capt. Richard Henry Lee, 281 acres 3 rod and 4 pole of land lying near the lower end of Yeocomico Neck in the County aforesaid beginning at angle "A" an old stump called Bonum's corner, the stock is between a black gum bearing north of and a large white oak bearing South the course from angle "A" to "B" as mentioned in the above plan at the figure 7 is a small dwelling house near the line at angle "B" is a stake in the old field near the gate leads to the mansion house of the widow Steptoe. At figure 8 is a tobacco house and stock houses about 10 foot within the line figure 9 the marsh gut at angle "C" [missing] stake in the corner field near a small mulberry [missing] Critcher in the above land at figure 2 is the first line till near the end of a lane that leads to Critcher's at figure 3 is a corner tree mentioned in the plan, at angle "E" in figure 4 is another corner tree mentioned in the plan at angle "F" and figure 9 is another corner tree mentioned in the plan at angle "C" is Capt. Newton's ditch. Surveyed by Peter Harlee
Westmoreland Sct. At a Court held for the said County the 25th day of July 1758
at this Court the said Richard Jackson, Daniel Tebbs and John Crabb returned their report that they had divided the land of the said James Steptoe, deceased between the complainants and respondents as will appear by the plot thereto annexed and that the rent of the said land is of the value of 15 pounds per annum from the death of the said James Steptoe and the said report being read it is further ordered adjudged and decreed that the said Complainants hold the lower part of the land where on the late dwelling house of the said James Steptoe now stands and that the respondents hold the upper part of the said land according to the dividing line in the said surveyors plat and that each party receive their proportion of the rent from the death of the said testator and that the plot in the report be recorded and it is also ordered that each party to pay their own cost.
Recorded the seventh day of August 1758   Test: George Lee CCW

1761 Westmoreland County, Virginia Deeds & Will Book 13, [Mike Marshall]; Page 166.
Lovell to Monroe Mortgage
This indenture made the 15 day of May 1758 between John Lovell the Parish of Washington in County of Westmoreland of the one part and John Monroe, William Bernard in James Blair of the Parish and County aforesaid of the other part. Whereas the said John Monroe, William Bernard and James Blair at the special instance and request of the said John Lovell sometime in the year 1755 became security to William Berryman, Gent., sheriff of the said County of Westmoreland for the

said John Lovell's new performance and execution of the office in trust of undersheriff in the County of Westmorland aforesaid and also for the payment of 33 pounds current money to the said William Berryman and where the said [missing] instance and reg [missing] in the year of 1757 bound himself as a security together with Samuel Love, Gent., in a bond to Philip Ludwell Lee and William Bernard, Gent., of the said County Westmoreland for the said John Lovell's due performance and execution of the office and trust of Parish collection. Now this indenture witness that as well for saving harmless the said John Monroe, William Bernard and James Blair and from all manner of suits judgments and executions by the said William Berryman against the said John Monroe, William Bernard and James Blair and by the said Philip Ludwell Lee and William Bernard against the said John Monroe and Samuel Love for and by means of several securities made and entered into in behalf of the said John Lovell as for the sum of five shillings to him in hand paid the receipt whereof he doth hereof acknowledge. He, the said John Lovell as granted bargain and sold by these presents unto John Monroe, and William Bernard and James Blair [the following; a tract of land whereon the said John Lovell now lives which was part of the tract belonging to Robert Lovell, father to the said John Lovell called Bluff Point in Westmoreland County; one yoke of oxen, two cows and calves, six leather chairs, one couch, 3 feather beds, a bay horse called Pritchett, a gray mare, one mullato called Harry, and one black walnut table. Provided nevertheless that if the said John Lovell shall save harmless and keep indemnified John Monroe, William Bernard and James Blair from all such suits judgments executions payments on payments or any sum of money or quantity of tobacco by means of their several suretyships [missing] Philip Ludwell Lee and William Bernard [missing] request of the said John Lovell as aforesaid and shall procure on or before the first day of February 1759 under the hand and seals of the said William Berryman and Philip Ludwell Lee and William Bernard him proper discharges and defenses against the before recited bonds entered into severally and respectively payable to them that then and from thence forth this present indenture and the estate hereby made shall cease. In witness whereof I have hereunto set my hand and seal this state and year first above written.
Signed sealed and acknowledged in presence of   John Lovell
Hopkins Rankins (his mark)
Burditt Stephens (his mark)
Jacob Lovell
George Finch (his mark)
Westmoreland Sct. At a Court held for the said County the 25 July 1758 this mortgage of land and other things therein mentioned passed from John Lovell to John Monroe, William Bernard and James Blair was proved in court by the oath of Hopkins Rankins, Burditt Stephens and George Finch three of the witnesses thereto and ordered to be recorded.
Recorded 31st day of July 1758   Test: George Lee CCW

Page 168.
Rochester & wife to Rust Lease
This indenture made the 29th day of August 1757 between William Rochester and Mary Rochester his wife of the Parish of Cople and County of Westmoreland of one part and Peter Rust of the parish and county aforesaid of the other part. Witnesseth that William Rochester and Mary Rochester his wife in consideration of 5 shillings has sold unto Peter Rust all that plantation tract of land containing 100 acres and being in Yeocomico forest where Mary Hopwood now lives being part of a tract of land formerly granted to William Walker and sold by William Walker, Jr., to Samuel Earle as by deed bearing date July 10th, 1672 and by Earle sold to Thomas Durrant and afterwards became the property of Richard Hopwood who by his last will gave the land to his son Moses Hopwood who sold the land to Thomas Asbury, deceased who gave the land to his daughter Mary Asbury as by his will doth appear; and binding upon the land of William Bailey, on the land of John Graham, Northwest to the said Rust's Mill Pond and thence up the mill pond and run to the land of Thomas Bennett, then down Bennett's line to the aforesaid land of Bailey. To Peter Rust from the day of the date of these presents from and during the term of one whole year thence next ensuing yielding and paying the rent of one ear of Indian corn on the last day of said term if demanded to the intent that by virtue of these presents and of the statute for transferring uses into possession he the said Peter Rust may be in actual possession of the premises. In witness whereof the said

parties to these presents have interchangeably set their hands and seals the day and year first above written.

Sealed and delivered in presence of   William Rochester
James Balfour   Mary Rochester
John Fisher (his mark)
Robert Newgin (his mark)

Westmoreland Sct. At a Court held for the said County the 29th day of September 1757 this deed of lease for lands passed from William Rochester and Mary Rochester his wife to Peter Rust was acknowledged in court by the said Mary Rochester being first privily examined, relinquished her right of dower and inheritance to the deed ordered to be lodged. Test: George Lee

Page 171.
Rochester & Wife to Rust Indenture
This indenture made the 13th day of August 1757 between William Rochester and Mary Rochester his wife of the Parish of Cople and County of Westmoreland of the one part and Peter Rust of the parish and county aforesaid of the other part. Witnesseth that William Rochester and Mary Rochester his wife in consideration of 3500 pounds of tobacco has sold unto Peter Rust in his actual possession now being by virtue of a bargain and sale to him paid for one whole year by indenture bearing date the day next before the date of the date of these presents and by the force of the statute for transferring uses into possession assigns forever all that plantation containing 100 acres lying in Yeocomico forrest [same description page 168]. In witness whereof the said parties to these presents have interchangeably set their hands and seals this day and year first above written.

Sealed and delivered in presence of   William Rochester
James Balfour   Mary Rochester
John Fisher (his mark)
Robert Newgent (his mark)

Westmoreland Sct. At a Court held for the said County the 29th day of September 1757 this deed of deed for lands passed from William Rochester and Mary Rochester his wife to Peter Rust was acknowledged in court by the said Mary Rochester will being first privily examined relinquished her right of dower and inheritance to the the deed ordered to be lodged. Test: George Lee CCW
Westmoreland Sct. At a Court held for the said County on the 29th day of August 1758 William Rochester came into Court and personally acknowledged this release of land by him passed to Peter Rust to be his proper act and deed and then ordered to be recorded.
Recorded the first day of September 1758   Test: George Lee CCW

Page 175.
Garner to Garner Lease
This indenture made the 31st day of July 1758 between Abraham Garner of the County of Westmoreland, planter of the one part and Joseph Garner of the same County, planter of the other part. Witnesseth that Abraham Garner in consideration of the rents and covenants and services hereafter mentioned hath demised granted let to farm let unto Joseph Garner, 80 acres of land lying in Ragged Point Neck and bounded as followeth; beginning at a small marked sweet gum at the head of a cove near Haw Point and running along by a straight line were now my orchards fence runs, and from thence to a small marked cedar tree by the roadside that leads to my house and from thence to a small marked white oak and to continue the same course from thence to another small marked white oak tree in the corner of an old field and from thence to a persimmon tree marked also and from thence along the old field as it now runs to a marked hickory tree and from thence to two persimmon trees marked at the head of a cove to a point formerly called Bradley's Point, and so along as the land binds on the creek to Scutt's Point and thence up a large cove belonging [missing] aforesaid first beginning [missing] 80 acres more or less.
To have and to hold the said plantation land and premises with all appurtenances unto him the said Joseph Garner, Catherine Garner his wife and Nathaniel Garner their son and the longest liver of them yielding and paying yearly and every year and to the said Abraham Garner the 25th day of December the full sum and quantity of 1000 pounds of crop tobacco and cask only the first year

Westmoreland County, Virginia Deeds & Wills DB13, 1756-1761

excepted which he is to have rent free in consideration whereof he to build a dwelling house and tobacco house with the liberty of getting timber on any part of said land. In witness whereof the said parties have hereunto set their hands and seals the day and year first written.

Signed sealed and delivered in the presence of   Abraham Garner
Johnn Norwood, John Brown   Joseph Garner (his mark)

Westmoreland Sct. At a Court held for the said County the 29th day of August 1758 Abraham Garner came into court and personally acknowledged this lease of land by him passed to Joseph Garner also their bond for performance of covenants to be their proper act and deeds which at the instance of the said Joseph were admitted to record.
Recorded the fifth day of September 1758   Test: George Lee CCW

Page 178.
Ashton from Hudson
This Indenture made the 7th day of August 1758 between Rush Hudson of the county of Orange, planter of the one part and Burditt Ashton of the Parish of Washington and County of Westmoreland, Gent., in consideration of the sum of 5 pounds current money current money of Virginia has sold a tract of land lying in the Parish of Washington and County of Westmoreland containing 25 acres and bounded northerly and westerly by the land and plantation of Burditt Ashton, easterly by land purchased by the said Ashton of Richard Haikes and northerly by lands in possession of Elizabeth Settle and one other parcel of land purchased of Valentine Hudson by the said Burditt Ashton which said tract to be sold was given and devised by Joshua Hudson to his sons Valentine Hudson and Rush Hudson describing it to be the remaining part of his land lying between John Hudson and Joshua Hudson to be equally divided between them, his son Valentine Hudson to have his first choice as said will remaining on record may full appear. In witness whereof the said Rush Hudson has set his hand and seal this day and year above written.

Signed and acknowledged in presence of   Rush Hudson
William Bernard
Original Wroe
William Monroe
John Ashton

Westmoreland Sct. At a court held for the said county the 29th day of August 1758 this deed of sale and consideration thereon endorsed passed from Rush Hudson to Burditt Ashton was proved by the oaths of all the witnesses which on motion of the said Ashton were admitted to record.
Recorded the 5th day of September 1758   Test: George Lee CCW

Page 180.
Steptoe v Steptoe Division of Dower Land
Westmoreland Sct. At a court held for the said county the 25th day of July 1758, on the motion of Mrs. Elizabeth Steptoe, widow of Col. James Steptoe, deceased and by consent of the executors of the said James, it is ordered that Samuel Oldham, Daniel Tebbs, John Newton & Peter Rust or any three of them do allot unto the said Elizabeth her lawful dower of the said deceased lands in the county and report their proceedings therein to the next court to be held for the said County. Copy Test: George Lee CCW

Page 180.
Steptoe v Steptoe Plat & Survey
Westmoreland Sct. In obedience to an order of the Westmoreland court, we the subscribers did meet [at the house of] James Steptoe, deceased, together [missing] Elizabeth Steptoe, his widow, her dower or third part of the said Steptoe's land in the manner following; Beginning on Potomac River side at the corner of Mr. George Jeffries land and running along his line 99 poles to a white oak in the said Jeffries line, thence extending across the tract North 32-1/2° West 307 pole, to a sweet gum in the line of Captain Peter Rust near the head of a branch thence down the said branch and crossing a large marsh along the said Rust's line to a large hickory on the edge of the said marsh thence South 86° East 24 poles to a hickory on the River Side thence down the said river the several courses and meanders thereof to the beginning containing 190 acres of land as

may appear by the surveyors plat hereto annexed. Given under our hands and seals this 3rd day of August 1758.
Samuel Oldham
Daniel Tebbs
John Newton
[Surveyor's Platt follows bottom of page 181]
Surveyed and divided 320 acres of land in Westmoreland County lying on the Potomac River formerly the land of Col. James Steptoe, deceased and laid off to Mrs. Steptoe, widow, 190 acres binding on the river side, beginning at the letter "A" where is the corner of George Jeffries land and running along his line 99 pole to a white oak at "B" thence North 32-1/2° West 307 pole to a sweet gum at the letter "C" in the line of Captain Peter Rust near the head of a branch thence down the branch and crossing a large marsh along the said Rust's line to the letter "D" at the edge of the marsh thence South 86° East 24 pole to a large hickory on the river side thence down the several meanders thereof to the beginning. The orphan has 251 of land lying some distance from this parcel and these 130 acres makes up his part 381 and the widow has only her thirds of the whole which is 571 acres, the line "H-I" is a crooked ditch and did not run, that's only calculated by the courses of the patent "F" a corner white oak to Lowe "G" another corner gum to Lowe "H" a maple "J" is an old mulberry corner to Rust surveyed and completed the 3rd day of August 1758.
William Garland
Westmoreland Sct. At a court held for the said county the 29th day of August 1758 this report and allotment of Mrs. Elizabeth Steptoe's dower of land of her late husband James Steptoe, Gent., deceased together with the plat and surveyors report was returned unto court and ordered to be recorded.
Recorded the 6th day of September 1758   Test: George Lee CCW

Page 183.
Brown's Will
The will and testament of Original Browne being in perfect memory is as follows.
Item I give and bequeath unto my loving wife Elizabeth Browne all my lands and Negroes household goods and other chattles whatsoever both movable and immovable to her at her disposal. Also, I leave to her my whole and sole executrix of this my last will and testament.
I have unto set my hand and affixed my seal this 29th day of January 1744.
Signed sealed and delivered in the presence of us   Original Browne
John Piper
John Jett
Abraham Blagg
Westmoreland Sct. At a Court held for the said County the 29th day of November 1757 this last will and testament of Original Browne was proved by the oath of John Piper and Abraham Blagg the surviving witnesses thereto and ordered to be lodged for the executrix to qualify.
Test: George Lee CCW
Westmoreland Sct. At a Court held for the said County the 29th day of August 1758 this last will and testament of Original Browne been presented into Court and November last and proved by John Piper Abraham Blagg the surviving witnesses and then lodged for the executrix to qualify in it being now in the corn executrix would not take upon her the burden of the execution of the said will, on motion of David Craig and his performing all such things as the law in such cases require administration of all and singular the goods and chattels of the said Original Browne, deceased the will annexed are in due form granted him.
Recorded the sixth day of September 1758   Test: George Lee CCW

Page 184.
Beard to Hilton Indenture
This indenture made the 26th day of September 1750 between John Beard the Parish of Washington in County of Westmoreland, planter of the one part and John Hilton of the parish and County aforesaid the other part. Witnesseth the said John Beard in consideration of the sum of 100 pounds current money has sold to John Hilton a tract of land in the said Parish of Washington in

County of Westmoreland containing by estimation 150 acres, which land is the northernmost part of a tract of land granted to John Beard by patent bearing date the 23rd day of March 1664 which said tract of land after the death of the said John Beard descended in fee to his son John Beard his heir at law and by the last will and testament of the said John Beard, the son, given and disposed of in the following manner, that is to say, to his son George Beard 200 acres part thereof including the plantation on which he then lived and to his son John Beard, party to these presents, the residue thereof on that side whereof John Lansdown lived. In witness whereof the said John Beard hath hereunto his set his hand and seal the day and year above written.   John Beard

Westmoreland Sct. At a Court held for the said County the 26th day of September 1758 John Beard came into Court and personally acknowledged this deed for land also the receipt for the consideration thereon endorsed by him passed to John Hilton to be his proper act and deed which on motion of the said Hilton or admitted to record.
Recorded the 10th day of October 1758   Test: George Lee CCW

Page 185.
Neale Jr. to Cranford Lease
This indenture made the 3rd day of June 1758 between Daniel Neale, Jr., of the County of Westmoreland, planter of the one part and Thomas Crawford, weaver of the same County of the other part. Witnesseth the said Daniel Neale, Jr., in consideration of the yearly rents and covenants customized lease and to farm let unto Thomas Crawford for the term of 14 years from Christmas Day next, 40 acres of land being the plantation whereon the said Thomas Crawford now lives including the dwelling house and other houses paying yearly [missing] 40 shillings in [missing] having for the said Neale's family at [missing] weavers [missing].
Signed Sealed delivered in the presence of   Daniel Neale, Jr.
William Pierce   Thomas Crawford (his mark)
John Spence,
James Browne

Westmoreland Sct. At a Court held for the said County the 26th day of September 1758 this deed of lease for lands passed from Daniel Neale, Jr., to Thomas Crawford was proved by the oath of William Pierce, John Spence, and James Brown the witnesses thereto subscribed and on motion of the said Crawford were admitted to record.
Recorded the 10th day of October 1758   Test: George Lee CCW

Page 187.
Vickers to Triplett Lease
This indenture made the 2nd day of June 1758 between John Vickers of the Parish of Dettingen in County of Prince William of one part and John Triplett of Hanover Parish in the County of King George of the other part. Witnesseth that John Vickers [Vicars] in consideration of five shillings has sold unto John Triplett a tract of land containing 63 acres situated in the Parish of Washington in County of Westmoreland formerly the land belonging to Elias Webb together with all the rights members and appurtenances yielding and paying the rent of one ear of Indian corn on the last day of the said term if demanded to the intent and purpose that by virtue of these presents and of the statute for transferring uses into possession he the said John Triplett may be in the full and actual possession of the premises and thereby be the better enabled to accept and take a grant and release of the reversions and inheritance thereof to him and his heirs. In witness whereof the parties to these presents have set his hands and seals the day and year first above written.
Signed sealed and delivered in the presence of   John Vickers (his mark)
Elias Hore, George Calvert
James Triplett, William Triplett

Westmoreland Sct. At a Court held for the said County the 26th day of September 1758 this deed of lease for land passed from John Vickers to John Triplett was proved in court by the oath of Elias Hore, James Triplett and William Triplett three of the witnesses thereto subscribed and on motion of the said Triplett were admitted to record
Recorded the 11th day of October 1758   Test: George Lee CCW

Page 188.
Vickers to Triplett Indenture
This indenture made the third day of June 1758 between John Vickers of the Parish of Dettingen in County of Prince William of one part and John Triplett of Hanover Parish in the County of King George of the other part. Witnesseth that John Vickers [Vicars] in consideration of 8 pounds current money of Virginia has released unto John Triplett in his actual possession now being by virtue of a bargain and sale to him thereof made for one whole year by indenture having date the day next before the date of the date of these presents and by force of the statute for transferring uses into possession and to his heirs and assigns that tract of parcel of land containing 63 acres more or less Scituate in the Parish of Washington in the County of Westmoreland. In witness whereof the said party to these presents have set his hand and seal the day and year first above written.
Signed sealed and delivered in the presence of   John Vickers (his mark)
Elias Hore, George Calvert
James Triplett, William Triplett
Westmoreland Sct. At a Court held for the said County the 26th day of September 1758 this deed of release for land together with the receipt thereon endorsed passed from John Vickers to John Triplett was proved in court by the oath of Elias Hore, James Triplett and William Triplett three of the witnesses thereto subscribed and on motion of the said Triplett were admitted to record
recorded the 11th day of October 1758   Test: George Lee CCW

Page 190.
Garner to Lowe Deed of Lease
This indenture made this 12th August in 1758 between Jeremiah Garner of the County of Westmoreland, planter of the one part and Richard Lowe of the county aforesaid in consideration of 10 pounds current money of Virginia has demised lease let and to farm let unto Richard Lowe one full fourth part of the land and premises the said Jeremiah Garner purchased of William Dunbar by deed made and acknowledged in 1754 and now in possession of Richard Lowe by a division lately made. In witness whereof the parties to these presents have set their hands and seals the day and year first above written.
Signed Sealed and delivered in presence of   Jeremiah Garner
Richard Moore   Richard Lowe
Richard Fuller
Elijah Moxley (his mark)
Westmoreland Sct. At a Court held for the said County the 28th day of November 1758 this deed of lease for land passed from Jeremiah Garner to Richard Lowe was proved in court by the oath of the witnesses thereto subscribed and thereupon ordered to be recorded
recorded the 5th day of November 1758   Test: George Lee CCW

Page 192.
Davis to Spark Lease
Indenture made the 11th day of July 1758 between Thomas Davis, Elizabeth Davis his wife and John Davis his son the County of Westmoreland and Parish of Washington the one part and Alexander Spark of the Parish of Cople and County aforesaid the other part.
Whereas by one indenture of lease bearing date the seventh day of November 1745 made between Robert Vaulx of the County of Westmoreland in Parish of Washington of the one part and the said Thomas Davis, Elizabeth Davis his wife and John Davis his son on the other part for the considerations therein mentioned did demise, grant and to farm let unto the said Thomas Davis and his wife and son a tenement of land lying in the County of Westmoreland and Parish of Washington from the seventh day of November during the term of natural lives of the said Thomas Davis and his wife and son paying the yearly rent of 530 pounds of tobacco and two fat capons and the quit rents thereof upon the 25th day of December every year unto the said Robert Vaulx. Now this indenture witnesseth that the said Thomas Davis, Elizabeth Davis his wife and John Davis his son conjointly and severally and in consideration of 20 pounds lawful currency hath assigned by these presents to Alexander Spark the aforesaid tenement of land for the said term lives which is yet to come and unexpired. In witness whereof we have hereunto set our hands and seals this day and

date above-mentioned presence of
Thomas Minor
Thomas Davis, Jr.
William Taylor
Thomas Davis
Elizabeth Davis (her mark)
John Davis

Westmoreland Sct. At a Court held for the said County the 28th day of November 1758 this deed of land passed from Thomas Davis, Elizabeth Davis his wife and John Davis to Alexander Spark was acknowledged in court by the said Thomas Davis and John Davis.
Thomas Minor and Thomas Davis, Jr., made oath that they saw the said Elizabeth Davis signed the said deed and on motion of the said Spark were ordered to be recorded.
Recorded the 17th day of November 1758   Test: George Lee CCW

Page 195.
Robinson from Pettit Indenture
This indenture made the 20th day of November 1758 between John Pettit of the Parish of Washington and the County of Westmoreland, Gent., of the one part and Maximilian Robinson of the Parish of Hanover and the County of King George and colony of Virginia, Gent., of the other part. Witnesseth that the said John Pettit in consideration of 800 pounds current money of Virginia has sold Maximilian Robinson all that plantation tract containing by estimation 760 acres being in the Parish of Washington and County of Westmoreland and is bounded according to the deeds made by Thomas Shaw for the said quantity of 760 acres by deeds of lease and release having date the 4 November 1754 which said plantation is where the said John Pettit now dwells; also all that plantation and land were Richard Steele formerly lived containing by estimation 200 acres bounded as reported which said land was set up to public sale to the highest bidder as directed by the will of Weedon Arnold, deceased and purchased by the said John Pettit and his joying to the aforementioned 760 acres and all houses woods ways waters and watercourses profits commodities and advantages whatsoever belonging. In witness whereof the said John Pettit has hereunto set his hand and seal this day and year above written
sealed and delivered in the presence of us   John Pettit
David Morrison
Henry Fauntleroy
Mary Nicholson
Thomas Morris

Westmoreland Sct. At a Court held for the said County the 28th day of November 1758 John Pettit acknowledge this deed [missing] endorsed to Maximilian Robinson to be his proper act and deed which on motion of the said Robinson are ordered to be record
recorded the 20th day of December 1758   Test: George Lee CCW

Page 197.
Roe to Monroe
This indenture made the 24th day of June 1758 between Henry Roe of Washington Parish in Westmoreland County, planter of the one part and Andrew Monroe, Jr., of the same county and parish of the other part. Witnesseth the said Henry Roe in consideration of the annual rent of one thousand pounds crop tobacco clear of cask and quit rents has farm let a tenement of land to Andrew Monroe, Jr., lying in Westmoreland County and bounded as followeth; beginning at a Pock [ironwood tree] by the main road on the line of Capt. William Monroe, running from thence southwardly to a locust, thence to a marked by the wheat patch formerly belonging to Bunch Roe, deceased, thence round several courses to the aforesaid beginning so as to include 100 acres of land with a house to be built thereon 16 ft.² with an outside chimney. To have and to hold the land with all its rights from the day of the date hereof during the term of eight years to be fully completed and handed yielding and paying to the said Henry Roe the annual rent after the 25th day of March.
Signed sealed delivered in the presence of   Henry Roe
James Bankhead   Andrew Monroe, Jr.
Lovell Harrison
Spence Monroe
Westmoreland Sct. At a Court held for the said County the 28th day of November 1758 this deed of

lease for land passed from Henry Roe to Andrew Monroe, Jr., was proved in court by the oath of James Bankhead, Lovell Harrison and Spence Monroe the witnesses thereto subscribed and thereupon ordered to be recorded.
Recorded the 10th day of January 1759   Test: George Lee CCW

Page 199.
Wroe & Wife to Pope
This indenture made the 10th day of November 1758 between William Wroe and Elizabeth Wroe his wife of the Parish of Washington in County of Westmoreland of the one part and Nathaniel Pope, son and heir at law to the said Elizabeth Wroe of the County of Louisa of the other part. Witnesseth that William Wroe and Elizabeth Wroe his wife is for the natural love and affection which they have to the said Nathaniel Pope and five shillings have given him a tract of land lying in the Parish of Washington in County of Westmoreland containing by estimation 515 acres. Bounded as followeth northerly by Potomack [missing] possession of [missing] Daniel McCarty of Thomas Shaw and William Bridges of which said tract of land a certain Thomas Pope of County of Bristol was seized in fee simple and being seized thereof on the third day of September 1684 being bound on voyage to see did give and devise his son Thomas Pope the above described lands and premises and to the heirs of his body lawfully begotten and for want of such issue to his two sons Charles Pope and Nathaniel Pope equally as tenants in common, from which said voyage the said Thomas Pope the father having never returned, the said Thomas Pope entered and was therefore seized as tenant in fee tail and soon after departed this life leaving issue Mary Pope his only daughter and heiress at law, who intermarried with Samuel Randall of the County of Cork, merchant and sometime on or about the year 1730 departed this life intestate and without heirs upon whose death without issue aforesaid the said tract of land descended and came to Nathaniel Pope who devisee in remainder and son of the said Thomas Pope the testator in fee simple the other devisee in remainder the said Charles Pope being also dead, intestate and without issue which said Nathaniel Pope the devisee in remainder as aforesaid having also departed this life intestate the said tract of land descended and came to the said Elizabeth Wroe party to these presents in fee simple as his only daughter and heiress at law together with all and singular the appurtenances the said tract of land.
In witness whereof the said William Wroe and Elizabeth Wroe his wife have hereunto set their hands and seals the day and year above written.
Signed sealed and acknowledged in presence of   William Wroe
William Bernard   Elizabeth Wroe (her mark)
William Degge
James Degge
Westmoreland Sct. At a Court held for the said County the 28th day of November 1758 this deed of land passed from William Wroe and Elizabeth Wroe his wife to Nathaniel Pope was proved in court by the oath of the witnesses thereto subscribed also the receipt for the consideration thereon endorsed and on motion of the said Pope was therefore ordered to be recorded
recorded the 10th day of January 1759   Test: George Lee CCW

Page 201.
Bennett's Will
In the name of God Amen, I William Bennett of Westmoreland County being sick and weak of body but of perfect sense and memory do make and ordain this my last will and testament in manner and form following.
Item I give to my dear and loving mother Elizabeth Bennett my horse called Deely and all my money and debts which are due to me for and during her natural life. And after her death the same to my loving brother Charles Bennett.
Item I give to my loving brother Daniel Bennett all my joyners and carpenters tools.
Item I give to my loving brother Charles Bennett my chest, wearing apparel and all other things which is my own property except the things before given.
Item I leave my loving brother Thomas Bennett and Daniel Bennett executors of this my last will and testament.
In witness whereof I have hereunto set my hand and seal this 18th day of September 1758

Westmoreland County, Virginia Deeds & Wills DB13, 1756-1761

Signed Sealed and delivered in the presence of us   William Bennett
Matthew Partridge
John Butler
Solomon Bennett
Westmoreland Sct. At a Court held for the said County the 30th day of January 1759 this last Will and Testament of William Bennett, deceased was presented into Court by Thomas Bennett and Daniel Bennett the executors therein named who made oath thereto and being duly proved by the oath of John Butler and Solomon Bennett two of the witnesses thereunto subscribed is admitted to record in upon the motion of the said executors and their performing what the law in such cases require certificate is granted them for obtaining a probate thereof in due form.
Recorded the first day of February 1759   Test: George Lee CC W

Page 203.
Eskridge to Tebbs Indenture
This indenture made the 16th day of January 1759 between Charles Eskridge of the County of Fairfax of the one part and Daniel Tebbs of the Parish of Cople and County of Westmoreland of the other part. Witnesseth that Charles Eskridge in consideration of the sum of 312 pounds current money of Virginia has sold to Daniel Tebbs a tract of land containing 195 acres being part of a tract of land given by the will of George Eskridge, Gent., deceased, bearing date the 27th day of October 1735 to Samuel Eskridge, father of the said Charles Eskridge and bounded as follows; beginning at a fork Maple corner, to the land of the orphans of Col. James Steptoe, deceased, extending along a crooked ditch North 1 ½° West 31 poles North 4° East 22 poles, North 3 ½° West 18 poles, North 3 ½° 86 poles, North 14 poles, South 11 ¼°, East 23 poles, North 24 ½°West 4 pole, to a mulberry in Capt. Peter Rust line, thence South 45° West 82 pole to a stump he corner tree of a ditch, thence along the edge South 70°, West 71 pole, to a stake, thence South 11 ½° East 100 pole to the corner of another ditch, thence South 9° West 200 pole to a Creek known by the name of Ward's Creek, thence down the several meanders thereof to the mouth of Kings Creek, thence up the third Creek and branch to the beginning. In witness whereof the said Charles Eskridge hath hereunto set his hand and affixed his seal the day and year first above written
Signed Sealed and delivered in the presence of   Charles Eskridge
Peter Rust
William Dunbar
Ashton Hall
Daniel Tebbs, Jr.
Memorandum that on the 16th day of January 1759 Charles Eskridge made livery and seizen of the lands and appurtenances within mentioned by delivery of turf and trigg and the ring of the door of the chief mansion house of the lands within mentioned unto Daniel Tebbs. In the name of the whole lands and appurtenances within granted bargained and sold according to the tenure and effect of the within deed.
In the presence of
Peter Rust
William Dunbar
Ashton Hall
Daniel Tebbs, Jr.
Westmoreland Sct. At a Court held for the said County the 27th day of February 1759 this deed of feoffment passed from Charles Eskridge to Daniel Tebbs together with the livery and seizen and receipt thereon endorsed was proved by the oaths of Ashton Hall, Peter Rust and Daniel Tebbs, Jr., three of the witnesses thereto subscribed also the commission for the privy examination of Hannah Eskridge the wife of Charles being returned that she was thereto consenting were both ordered to be recorded.
Recorded the 5th day of March 1759   Test: George Lee CCW

Page 206.
Eskridge to Tebbs Privy Examination
To John Carlisle, Robert Adams and John Hunter of Fairfax County, Gent., greetings. Whereas

Charles Eskridge by a certain indenture of feoffment bearing date the 17th day of January 1759 has conveyed unto Daniel Tebbs of the County of Westmorland the fee simple estate of 195 acres of land lying in the Parish of Cople. And whereas Hannah Eskridge the wife of the said Charles Eskridge cannot conveniently come to the said court to acknowledge the conveyance. Therefore, we do give unto you or any two of you power to receive the acknowledgment which the said Hannah Eskridge shall be willing to make.
Witness George Lee, clerk of our county court the 16th day of January.   George Lee CCW
Fairfax County February 9, 1759
in obedience to the above order of Court the subscribers have privately examined Mrs. Hannah Eskridge will of her own free will and accord relinquished her right and title to the above mentioned land and desires of the same may be recorded in the above court of Westmoreland as witness our hands and seals dated above
Robert Adams,
John Hunter
Westmoreland Sct. At a Court held for the said County the 24th day of February 1759 this commission for the privy examination of Hannah Eskridge wife of Charles Eskridge for relinquishment of her right of dower and inheritance to the land her husband sold to Daniel Tebbs her consenting was ordered to be recorded. Test: George Lee CCW

Page 208.
Connelly's Dower Allotted
Westmoreland Sct. Pursuant to an order of the court held for ye said county the 29th of November 1758, we whose names are underwritten being appointed by the said court to allot Mary Connelly relict and administratrix of Henry Asbury, deceased her lawful dower in the lands and have allotted ye same as followeth; vizt; beginning at a chestnut tree standing in the line that divides this land from the land of Thomas Wright and from thence along a line of marked trees to the head of a branch, thence down the said branch to the Double Mill Pond, the land on the north side of the branch which we allot for her dower in the said lands being formerly known by the name of John Dowsitt's tract. Given under our hands this 5th day of January 1759.
Bennedict Middleton
Gerrard Hutt
Gerrard Hutt, Jr.
Westmoreland Sct. At a court held for the said county the 24th day of January 1759 this return of Mary Connelly's dower in Henry Asbury's land was returned into court and ordered to be recorded. Recorded the 12th day of February 1759.   Test: George Lee CCW

Page 208.
Hardwick & wife to Hutt
This indenture made the 21st day of February 1759 between Thomas Hardwick and Elizabeth Hardwick his wife of the Parish of Cople in County of Westmoreland, Planter of one part and Gerard Hutt of the aforesaid Parish in County of the other part. Witnesseth Thomas Hardwick and Elizabeth Hardwick his wife in consideration of 170 pounds current money of sold to Gerard Hutt all that plantation containing 180 one acres of land in the Parish of Cople in County of Westmoreland being the plantation whereon James Hardwick formerly lived father of Thomas Hardwick party to these presents and said land adjoining to the land of Thomas Blundell, deceased and Peyton's land. In witness whereof the said parties first above mentioned to these presents have interchangeably set their hands and seals the day and year first above mentioned.
Signed sealed and delivered in presence of us   Thomas Hardwick
Gerard Hutt, Jr.   Elizabeth Hardwick (her mark)
Joseph Redman
James Robinson
Westmoreland Sct. The 27th day of February 1759 Thomas Hardwick came in personally acknowledged this deed of feoffment together with the livery of seizen thereon endorsed to Gerard Hutt of to be his act and deed and Elizabeth Hardwick being first privily examined relinquished her right of dower to the same all of which on motion of the said Hutt ordered to be recorded.

Westmoreland County, Virginia Deeds & Wills DB13, 1756-1761

Recorded the 12th day of March 1759   Test: George Lee CCW

Page 211.
Neale's will
in the name of God Amen, the 28th eighth day of April 1758 I Daniel Neale of the Parish of Washington and County of Westmoreland being in perfect health but seriously considering the certainty of this transitory life do make this my last will and testament in manner and form.
Item I give and bequeath unto my four sons Christopher Neale, Presley Neale, Richard Neale, and John Neale, the following Negroes, to wit; Old Judah, Boson, Nan and her children called Mimaur, Tom and Sibley, Hany, Winey and her child called Nan, Lucy, a child called Conge and Harry a child; to be divided between them at the expiration of 10 years from the date of this present writing and it is further my will and desire that in case any of the said children should die without heirs that the said Negroes returned to the survivors of the four sons and not any part to my other children.
Item I give and bequeath unto my four sons above mentioned 20 pounds current money which I have now by me to be divided and to descend as the Negroes above me mentioned.
Item is my will and desire that the Negroes given to my sons Christopher Neale, Presley Neale, Richard Neale, and John Neale be kept together and worked for 10 years from the date hereof on my plantation I now live on in my plantation in Fairfax County at the discretion of my executors.
Item I give and bequeath unto my son Spence Neale plantation I now live on, likewise the half of my tract of land in Fairfax County to him and his heirs forever but my will is my son Spence Neale should die before he is of age and without a lawful heir the above mentioned lands to descend to my four youngest sons Christopher Neale, Presley Neale, Richard Neale, and John Neale.
Item I give to my son Spence Neale the following Negroes, to wit; Peter, Conge, Lucy and Dinah to him and his heirs lawfully begotten and for want of such heirs to be divided amongst my other children.
Item I give to my son Spence Neale by best feather bed and furniture, my grey horse and two cows and calves.
I give and bequeath unto my son Daniel Neale the other half of my tract of land in Fairfax County to him and his heirs forever and for want of such heirs to descend to my four sons Christopher Neale, Presley Neale, Richard Neale, and John Neale.
Item given to my son Daniel Neale one Negro girl called Betty, one Negro boy named James, and my bay riding mare to him and his heirs for want of such heirs to be divided amongst my other children.
Item I give and bequeath unto my son Rodham Neale whole of my lands in Richmond County to him and his heirs and for want of such heirs to descend to my four youngest sons Christopher Neale, Presley Neale, Richard Neale, and John Neale.
Item I give to my son Rodham Neale [missing] my bay horse to him and his heirs forever and for want of such heirs be divided amongst my other children.
Item I give unto my daughter Penny Spence Neale two Negro girls named Jean and Sarah, my gold ring, what clothes her deceased mother has left in the house, a black walnut chest and 20 pounds current money to be paid out of interest by my executors in paid her when she arrives to age of day of marriage to her and her heirs and for want of such heirs is my will and desire that the said Negroes and money be equally divided amongst my other children.
Item it is my will and desire that all the remainder of my estate not before by me given be equally divided amongst my children and;
lastly, I appoint my brother Edward Ransdell and my three sons Spence Neale, Daniel Neale and Rodham Neale to be my whole and sole executors of this my last will and testament.
Signed sealed published and delivered in the presence of   Daniel Neale
Edward Ransdell
Elizabeth Ransdell
Elizabeth Murphy
Westmoreland Sct. At a court held for the said County the 24th day of April 1759 this last will and Testament of Daniel Neale, deceased was presented into court by Edward and Spence Neale two of the executors therein named who made oath thereto and being also proved by the oath of Edward Ransdell, Elizabeth Ransdell, Elizabeth Murphy the witnesses thereto subscribed was

Westmoreland County, Virginia Deeds & Wills DB13, 1756-1761

ordered to be recorded and on motion of the said executors in the performing what the law in such cases require certificate was granted them for obtaining a probate in due form
recorded the 25th day of [missing] 1759   Test: George Lee CCW
[mm note: Edward Ransdell and Daniel Neale were half-brothers by their mother Ursula]

1761 Westmoreland County, Virginia Deeds & Will Book 13, [Mike Marshall]; Page 214.
Goff to Garner Lease
This indenture made this 30th day of November 1758, between Abraham Garner of the County of Westmoreland, planter of the one part and William O'Bryan Goff, Jane Goff his wife and Thomas O'Bryan Goff of the other part. Witnesseth that Abraham Garner in consideration of the rents and covenants has demised and to farm let unto William O'Bryan Goff, Jane Goff his wife and Thomas O'Bryan Goff part of a tract lying and being in Ragged Point Neck on Potomac River and bounded as follows; beginning at a persimmon tree near the head of a cove running up the plantation where on John Coombs now dwells being a cove belonging to Hurd's Creek [now Jackson's Creek] with a straight line across the river to the mouth of Hurd's Creek and up the said creek to the said cove and up the cove to the beginning persimmon tree containing 50 acres. To have and to hold the said land unto William O'Bryan Goff, Jane Goff his wife and Thomas O'Bryan Goff and the longest survivor of them paying yearly and every year unto Abraham Garner on the 25th day of December the full sum of 500 pounds of tobacco. In witness whereof the parties to these presents have interchangeably set their hands and seals this day and year first above mentioned.
Signed sealed and delivered in presence of   Abraham Garner
Ashton Hall   William O'Bryan Goff
Brian Cassiday (his mark)
Westmoreland Sct. At a court held for the said county the 24th day of April 1759 Abraham Garner came into court and personally acknowledged the lease for land by him passed to William O'Bryan Goff, Jane Goff to be his proper act and deed, which on motion of the said Goff was admitted to record.
Recorded the 25th day of April 1759   Test: George Lee CCW

Page 216.
Smith & Wife to Bailey
This indenture made the 16th day of October 1759 between James Smith and Mary Smith his wife of St. Stephen's Parish and county of Northumberland of the one part and James Bailey, Sr. of the Parish of Cople and County of Westmoreland of the other part. Witnesseth that James Smith and Mary Smith his wife in consideration of 2,850 pounds of tobacco clear of cask has sold to James Bailey, Sr. a tract of land containing 40 acres lying in the Parish of Cople and County of Westmoreland and adjoining the lands of James Bailey, Jr., and the lands of Robert Moon. In witness whereof the parties to these presents have interchangeably set their hands and seals this day and year first written.
Signed Sealed and delivered in presence of   James Smith (his mark)
James Bailey, Jr.
Daniel Winter
Peter Lamkin
Stephen Bailey
Westmoreland Sct. At a court held for the said county the 24th of April 1759 this deed of feoffment together with the livery of seizen thereon endorsed passed from James Smith and Mary Smith his wife to James Bailey Sr. was proved in court by the oaths of James Bailey Jr, Peter Lamkin and Stephen Bailey, three of the witnesses thereto and thereupon ordered to be recorded
Recorded the 26th day of April 1759   Test: George Lee CCW

Page 219.
Rochester's Division
Westmoreland Sct. Pursuant to two orders of the court held for the said county on the 29th day of August 1758 and the 26th day of September 1758 we whose names are underwritten being appointed by the said court to settle, adjust the assets of the estate of John Rochester, deceased

and to allot Thomas Critcher his wife's [Hester] lawful right of dower and each of the orphans their part of the said estate and all other the same as followeth; vizt; Bristow, Winny, Jennis, Bazlzuy and Lucy for her right of dower in the slaves and £18.6.6.4 in the personal estate, to wit; Sall, Bett, Hannah, Fortune, Jack, Ben, James [missing] £96.13.1. We also allot Thomas Critcher wife's dower or thirds in lands on the plantation, it being the land that lies on the [missing] side of the road [missing] leads from Mr. [missing] Simpson's Quarter to Ric[missing] Critcher?. Given under my hand and seal this 15th day of May 1759.
Benjamin Middleton
[Robert Middlton]
[Gerrard Hutt]
Westmoreland Sct. At a court held for the said county the 29th day of May 1759 the return of the division and dowery of the estate of John Rochester, deceased, was returned into court under the hands of the referees and ordered to be recorded, and the several claims to be processed with their proportionable parts according to the said report.
Recorded the 1st day of June 1759   Test: George Lee CCW

Page 219.
Tidwell to Palmer Sub-Lease
This indenture made the 14th day of June 1758 between John Tidwell of Cople Parish and County of Westmoreland of the one part and Thomas Palmer of the parish and county aforesaid of the other part. Witnesseth that John Tidwell in consideration of the yearly rents and covenants to be paid and performed hath demised and to farm let unto Thomas Palmer for and during the life of Robert Carter, Esq, his life part of the tract of land called "Brunts" lying and being in the Parish of Cople and County of Westmoreland and bounded as followeth, vizt; beginning in the branch that runs from "Brunts" and the first branch to a spring and from the spring up the branch to the head and then up the hill and across the hill unto the next nearest branch [missing] down the branch to the run that is the bounds that the said John Tidwell's lease on the [missing] Robert Carter, esq, down the run and to [missing] then up the branch [missing] bounds [missing] of the estate and other benefits together with all houses, edifices, profits, commodities, hereditaments and appurtenances. To have and to hold for and during the life of Robert Carter, Esq, yielding and paying yearly and every year unto John Tidwell the yearly rent of 450 pounds of lawful tobacco or 40 shillings quitrent money; paid on the 25th day of December every year. In witness whereof the parties to these presents have interchangeably set their hands and seals.
Signed Sealed and delivered in the presence of us   Thomas Palmer (his mark)
John White   John Tidwell
John Spence
Stephen Bailey (his mark)
Westmoreland Sct. At a court held for the said county the 29th day of May 1759 this lease of land passed from John Tidwell to Thomas Palmer was proved by the oaths of the witnesses thereto thereupon ordered to be recorded
Recorded the 1st day of June 1759   Test: George Lee CCW
[mm note: refer to 1754-1756 Westmoreland County, Virginia Deeds & Will Book 12, Page 148]

Page 221.
Smith & Wife to Baily Privy Examination
To William Taite Newton Keene & John John Foushee, Gent., greeting. Whereas James Smith of the county of Northumberland and Mary Smith his wife by their deed of feoffment bearing date 16th day of October 1758 conveyed unto James Baily of the County of Westmoreland the fee simple estate of 40 acres in the Parish of Cople and County of Westmoreland and Mary Smith cannot conveniently travel to our court to acknowledge the conveyance. Therefore, we do give you the power to personally receive her acknowledgement of the conveyance. Witness George Lee clerk of said county the 11 day of May 1759. George Lee CCW
By virtue of this commission this indenture of bargain and sale was acknowledged by Mary Smith at the Parish of St. Stephen's and county of Northumberland on the 26th day of May 1759 and that she was willing. The same recorded in the county court of Westmoreland.

Westmoreland County, Virginia Deeds & Wills DB13, 1756-1761

Before us
William Taite
Newton Keene
Westmoreland Sct. At a court held for the said county the 29th day of May 1759 this commission for the privy examination of Mary Smith wife of James Smith for relinquishment of her right of dower and inheritance of in and to the lands conveyed to James Bailey is ordered to be recorded.
Recorded the 1st day of June 1759   Test: George Lee CCW

Page 223.
Balling [Rallings] to Thompson
This indenture made the [xx] day of December 1759 between Samuel Rallings and Margaret Rallings his wife and Gladis Jett of the Parish of Washington and County of Westmoreland of the one part and James Thompson of the same parish of the other part. Witnesseth that Samuel Rallings and Margaret Rallings his wife and Gladis Jett in consideration of 80 pounds current money have sold unto James Thompson a tract of land containing 200 acres and lying in the Parish of Washington and County of Westmoreland on the north side of Mattox Creek being part of a patent granted unto William Smith by patent bearing date the 7th day of September 1695 and another part was granted unto William Freek by patent 11th day of September 1660 and another part of a patent granted to Ralph Faulkner bearing date the 4th day of March 1731/2; and is bounded as followeth, vizt; beginning at the creek opposite of the mouth of a branch, thence North to a live oak standing by the side of the branch, thence up a bridge to a main road that goes from the head of Mattox to Washington's Mill, thence up the said road to the second branch thence down the said branch to Price's line, thence with several courses of Price's line to the Wolf Trap Run thence down the run to Jett's Mill thence down the said path to a small red oak, thence South to the creek of a marked hickory to the creek to the beginning.
Signed sealed and delivered in the presence of   James Rallings
Original Wroe   Margaret Rallings
Thomas Robins
George Hailes (his mark)
John Triplett
John Jett (his mark)
Peter Jett
Gladis Jett (her mark)
Westmoreland Sct. At a court held for the said county the 29th day of May 1759 this deed of feoffment, together with the livery of seizen and receipt thereon endorsed passed from Samuel Rallings and Margaret Rallings his wife to James Thompson was proved by the oaths of John Triplett and George Hailes two of the witnesses thereto and ordered to be lodged for futher proof.
Test: George Lee CCW
Westmoreland Sct. At a court held for the said county the 30th day of May 1759 this deed of feoffment, together with the livery of seizen and receipt thereon endorsed passed from Samuel Rallings and Margaret Rallings his wife to James Thompson was fully proved by the oath of Orgina Wroe one of the witnesses thereto and ordered to be recorded.
Recorded the 1st day of June 1759   Test: George Lee CCW
[mm note: Gladis Spillman was the widow of John Jett.]

Page 223.
Balling [Rallings] to Thompson Privy Examination
To William Berryman, Archibald Campbell, John Monroe and James Blair, Gent., greeting Whereas Samuel Rallings and Margaret his wife of the County of Westmoreland by their indenture of feoffment bearing date 11th day of December 1758 have conveyed unto James Thompson of the said county the fee simple estate of 200 acres of land lying in the Parish of Washington and County of Westmoreland and whereas Margaret Rallings cannot conveniently travel to our court to make acknowledgement of the said conveyance; therefore we do give you the power to personally receive her acknowledgement of the conveyance. Witness George Lee clerk of the county the 22nd day of March 1759.

Page 68

By virtue of the within commission we the subscribers personally received the acknowledgement of Margaret Rallings wife of Samuel Ralllings and that she was willing. The same recorded in the county court of Westmoreland. Certified under our hands this 16th day of April 1759.
William Berryman
James Blair
Westmoreland Sct. At a court held for the said county the 30th day of May 1759 this commission for the privy examination of Margaret Rallings wife of Samuel Rallings for relinquishment of her right of dower and inheritance of in and to the lands conveyed to James Thompson is ordered to be recorded.
Recorded the 1st day of June 1759   Test: George Lee CCW

Page 227.
Bernard to Berryman Assignment
This indenture made the 16th day of October 1758 between John Monroe, William Bernard and James Blair, Gent., of the Parish of Washington and County of Westmoreland of one part and William Berryman, Gent., of the same parish and county of the other part. Witnesseth that whereas John Monroe, William Bernard and James Blair at the instance of John Lovell in 1755 had become security to William Berryman, sheriff of the County of Westmoreland for his diligent executor of the office and trust of under-sheriff in the county aforesaid and also for the payment of 33 pounds 6 shillings and 6 pence current money to the said William Berryman and whereas John Lovell in consideration John Monroe [William Bernard and James Blair] had become bound to [missing] save harmless and to [missing] indemnified the said John Monroe, William Bernard and James Blair of and from the payment of any sum or sums of money they might or should be liable for on account of their suretyship aforesaid set under mortgage in fee simple among other things a parcel of land which John Lovell then lived to John Monroe, William Bernard and James Blair which land was part of a tract belonging to Robert Lovell, father of John Lovell and by him given and conveyed to John Lovell by deed of gift as by indenture of mortgage bearing date the 15th day of May 1758. And whereas William Berryman since the execution of the said mortgage has purchased of Robert Lovell the remainder of the said tract of land and also hath agreed for and purchased of John Lovell the land and premises mentioned in the said indenture of mortgage or his, the said John Lovell's equity of redemption therein, and hath also covenanted granted and agreed to and with the said John Monroe, William Bernard and James Blair that William Berryman shall save harmless and keep indemnified the said John Monroe, William Bernard and James Blair from the payment of any sum or sums of money they may be liable for to William Berryman by means of their suretyship to John Lovell, provided the said sum of money which the said John Monroe, William Bernard and James Blair are or shall hereafter be obliged to pay, doth not exceed the sum of the purchase, to wit; 500 pounds current money for the whole tract purchased of Robert Lovell [missing] after deducting therefrom 150 pounds already paid [xx] said Robert Lovell and the said John Lovell's private debt to [xx] id William Amo [missing] 25 pounds or thereabouts. This Indenture [missing] the said John Monroe, William Bernard and James Blair [missing] and arguments have granted and released by these presents do grant and release unto William Berryman their right of foreclosure and all the right interest claim or demand whatsoever of them the said John Monroe, William Bernard and James Blair of in and to the said mortgaged lands and every part and parcel thereof. In witness whereof the said John Monroe, William Bernard and James Blair have hereunto set their hands and seals the day and year above written.
Signed Sealed and acknowledged n the presence of
John Ashton   John Monroe
Robert Lovell   William Bernard
Nathaniel Washington   James Blair
Westmoreland Sct.
At a court held for the said county the 28th day of November 1758
This deed of land together with the receipt thereon endorsed passed from John Monroe, William Bernard and James Blair to William Berryman was acknowledged by William Bernard and James Blair and lodged for acknowledgement. Test: George Lee
At a court held for the said county the 26th day of June 1759 this deed for land together with the

The condition of the above obligation is such that if the above bounded John Walker do in all things perform and fulfill the award and final determination of Mr. William Garland mutually elected and chosen by the said John Walker and Richard Walker to judge and determine controversies debates claims or demands or either of them hereto fore had particularly relating to a division of land in dispute between them so as the award and final determination to reduce into writing and signed by the said William Garland ready to be delivered to the said parties or such of them as shall devise the same on or before the 13th day of August next ensuing then this obligation to be void and of non-effect else to remain in full force and virtue.

Signed sealed and delivered in presence of us John Walker
John Bailey
William Garland

Page 238.
<u>Walker to Walker Surveyor's Plat & Report</u>
[Surveyor's Plat at top of page]
Surveyed and divided a certain piece of land for Richard Walker and John Walker in being in Westmoreland County and boarding on Yeocomico River. [missing] Richard Walker and John Walker now lives [missing] hold to a stake "B" thence South 58 ¼° West 205 poles to a red Oak at the letter "C", thence along a crooked line of marked trees near South 43° East 44 pole a line that divides this land from the land of Mr. Thomas Bennett to a corner of Flints Mill Creek at "D", thence the several meanders thereof to the beginning including 94 acres of land. John Walker's part begins at the letter "E" Back Creek, thence South 45° East five pole to a stake at the letter "B", thence the division line South 58 ½° West to a red oak standing on the side of a hill at the letter "C", thence North 4° West 117 poles to a red oak at "F" standing on the south side of Cool Springs Branch, thence down the several meanders thereof to the beginning including 94 acres of land. The said division being agreed on by the two brothers who entered a bond as may appear by record to stand to the same. John Bailey and James Bailey chain carriers being first sworn, surveyed and completed the 12th day of June 1759. William Garland
Westmoreland Sct. At a Court held for the said County the 28th day of August 1759 the above two arbitration bonds from Richard Walker and John Walker passed each to the other to stand to a division of land to be made by William Garland, together with the Plat and William Garland report was presented into Court and on the joint motion of the said Richard Walker and John Walker admitted to record.
Recorded 6 September 1759 Test: George Lee CCW

Page 239.
<u>Allerton's Will</u>
In the name of God Amen, I Willoughby Allerton of Westmoreland County being in sound mind and memory made this my last will and testament.
I give and bequeath to my wife Ann Allerton and her heirs forever one third part of all my lands and Negroes in Virginia or elsewhere in all my furniture in my house and out houses, my chaise and two horses that drives it, clear of any debts, legacies, or encumbrances
I give and bequeath to Mr. David Currie's two daughters, my sisters in law, Jane Currie and Alice Currie and their heirs forever the remaining two thirds parts of my land and Negroes in Virginia or elsewhere to be equally divided between them.
I give and bequeath to Capt. Hancock Eustace and his heirs forever after my debts are paid out of my personal estate in the Negroes given to my two sisters in law, Jane Currie and Alice Currie, the sum of 700 pounds current money.
I give and bequeath to Richard Lee Esq. and his heirs forever 100 acres of land adjoining his.
Lastly, I do constitute and appoint my friend Richard Lee Esq. and the Rev. Mr. David Currie executors of this my last will and Testament. Witness my hand and seal this 30th day of June 1759.
Signed sealed published in declared in the presence of us Willoughby Allerton
Clerkey Roukard? (her mark)
Ann McAuley (her mark)
Elizabeth Steptoe

Ane Currie
Richard Lee
Westmoreland Sct. At a court held for the said County the 25th day of September 1759 this last will and testament of Willoughby Allerton, Gent., deceased was presented into Court by David [Currie] and Richard Lee, Esq. the executors thereto and being proved by the oath of Clerkey Roukard, Anne McAuley], Elizabeth Steptoe, three of the witnesses thereto is admitted to record in upon motion of said executors and their performing what the law in such cases require certificate is granted them a probate thereof in due form.
Recorded this 29th day of September 1759   Test: George Lee

Page 241.
Piper's Will
In the name of God Amen by John Piper of Westmoreland County being sick and weak but of disposing sense and memory do make and constitute and ordain this my last will and testament.
I give and devise to my son-in-law William Monroe and his wife my daughter Rachael Monroe a tract of land whereon James Reynolds now lives adjoining the land of Thomas in George Monroe together with the four Negroes by the name of; Bassett, Milly, Nate and Beth and their several increase for and during their natural lives and after their decease to their heirs.
Item I give and devise to my son Jonathan Piper he tract of land containing 400 acres whereon he now resides together with the four Negroes by the name; James, Harry, Judy and James also in his possession for and during his natural life and after his decease one third part of the said land and Negroes to Ann Piper wife of Jonathan Piper if she should survive him. After the death of Jonathan Piper, the said land to descend to John Piper the eldest son Jonathan Piper.
Item whereas I have formally lent to my son Jonathan Piper the first household [missing] which he still continues to possess I now give [missing] Jonathan Piper forever the sundry property [missing].
Item [I give] to my son David Piper and his heirs forever the four Negroes following; Harry, Mamoth, Frank and Rem? being now in his possession together with the several stocks, household furniture &c which I had before only lent him.
Item I give to my son in law Thomas Muse and my daughter Ann Muse his wife for and during their natural lives in the life of the longest liver of them four Negroes named; Sarah, Jeto, Sall and Sias in after the decease of the survivor to the eldest son the said Ann Muse living in her death and for want of such to the daughter or daughters of the said Anne Muse living at her death. And in default of having either son or daughter living at her death then to my son William Piper, Benjamin Piper, and my daughter Mary Piper in their heirs forever.
I likewise give to my said son in law Thomas Muse two cows and calves, four ewes and lambs, two sows and pigs in 400 pounds of pork.
Item I give and devise to my son William Piper the plantation tract of land and mill whereon I now reside and if he should die without heir, I give the same to my son Benjamin Piper.
Item I give and devise to my son William Piper four Negroes] Lazarus, Pompy, Pender and Milly and a case of surveyor instruments and chains.
I give and devise to my son William Piper a tract of 100 acres whereon James Taylor now lives and which I purchased of Abraham Blagg.
Item Touching the provision for my youngest son Benjamin Piper, my will and desire isand I do hereby impower and direct my executors to make sale of and execute a proper deed for conveying lands lying in the county of Culpeper which I purchased of Capt. John Triplett for the most money that can be got and that he also make sale of a Negro named James in the possession of my son David Piper, together with a new set of cologn mill stones with the iron work belonging to the same. 40 head of sheep, twenty head of cattle at his discretion, and that with the money arising by the sale of the aforesaid articles together with what further provisions is hereafter made for [xxx] Benjamin Piper in money, my said executor do [missing] soon as he can with convenience [missing] on conveyance of which shall be in the name of my son Benjamin.
Item my will and desire further in touching the provisions for my son Benjamin Piper that my executor to the money arriving by the sale of the sundry particulars mentioned in the above devise, the money I have now in the house amounting to 260 pounds or thereabouts, together with the money arising from the sale of 1/2 my crop of tobacco now growing and that he invest the same

together with the above mentioned in the purchase of a tract of land aforesaid.
Item I give and bequeath to my son Benjamin Piper six Negroes; Sam, Joseph, Pegg, Mimy, Jenny and Patt.
I give and devise to my daughter Mary Piper five negroes; Luke, Cary, Peter, Isaac and Charity during her natural life and after her death to the heirs of her body or dying without issue to descend to my sons William Piper and Benjamin Piper.
Item my will and desire is that the residue of my estate, to wit; my household furniture and stock of different sort, be equally divided between my two sons William Piper and Benjamin Piper and my daughter Mary Piper.
Item my will and desire touching the disposition of the residue of my crop of tobacco is that my executor sell the same and first to discharge my debts and if there is any overplus to apply the same to the clothing if the negroes in my possession.
Item I appoint my son William Piper, guardian of my son Benjamin Piper and my daughter Mary Piper, maintaining their estates until they attain the age of 21 years.
Item my will is that the several negroes employed upon the plantation he continued thereon till the crop is finished.
Lastly, I appoint my son William Piper sole executor of this my last will and testament. In testimony whereof I have hereunto set my hand and seal this 12th day of August [17xx].
Signed Sealed and published in presence of us   John Piper
William Bernard
Peter Jett
William Spillman
John Spillman
Westmoreland Sct. At a court held for the said county the 25th day of September 1759 this last will and testament of John Piper, deceased was presented into court by his son William Piper, his executor therein named who made oath thereto and being proved by the oaths of William Bernard, Gent., Peter Jett and William Spillman, three of the witnesses thereto is admitted to record and upon motion of the executor and his performing what the law in such cases require, certificate is granted him for obtaining a probate thereof in due form.
Recorded the 29th day of September 1759   Test: George Lee CCW

Page 244.
Flood to Turberville Indenture
This indenture made the 25th day of September 1759 between William Flood, Gent., of the Parish of Cople and County of Westmoreland, of the one part and John Turberville, Gent., of the said parish and county of the other part. Witness that William Flood and Frances Flood his wife in consideration of 1,200 pounds current money of Virginia has sold to John Turberville several tracts contiguous and [missing] lying and being on and about [missing] the County of Westmoreland whereon the said William Flood formerly lived containing by estimation 800 acres. In witness whereof the parties to these presents have hereunto set their hand and seals this day and year first above written.
Sealed and delivered in the presence of us   William Flood
Joseph Peirce
L. Hipkins
Richard Parker
Westmoreland Sct. At a court held for the said county the 25th day of September 1759, William Flood, Gent., came into court and personally acknowledged, and together with the receipt thereon endorsed, this deed of land by him passed to John Turberville, Gent., which on motion of the said Turberville admitted to record.
Recorded the 1st day of October 1759   Test: George Lee CCW

Page 247.
Carr to Gardner Indenture
This indenture made the 8th day of February 1759 between Joseph Carr of the Parish of Truro and county of Fairfax, blacksmith of the one part and James Gregory, gardener the County of

Westmoreland and Parish of Cople of the other part. Witnesseth that Joseph Carr in consideration of 60 pounds current money of Virginia has sold to James Gregory a parcel of land that containing 100 acres that was given by the last will and Testament of William Carr to his daughter Anne Carr and afterwards given by the last will and testament of Joseph Carr to Joseph Remy in fee tail situate in the County of Westmoreland on the south side of the Double Mill Pond in joining on the land formerly the said William Carr's and now Joseph Lane and on the land of Henry Asbury and now the land of James Gregory. In witness whereof the parties to these presents have set their hands and seals the day month and year above written

Signed sealed and delivered in the presence of   Joseph Carr
James Lane, William Thomas
Thomas Connell, William Mathias
Elizabeth Thomas (her mark)
Elizabeth Lane (her mark)

Westmoreland Sct. At a Court held for said County the 29th day of May 1759 this deed of feoffment together with the livery of seizen and receipt thereupon endorsed, was proved by the oath of James Lane and Thomas Connell with the witnesses thereto and ordered to be lodged for further proof.
Test: George Lee CCW

Westmoreland Sct. At a Court held for said County the 25th day of September 1759 this deed of feoffment together with the livery of seizen and receipt thereupon endorsed, was fully proved by the oath of William Thomas a witness thereto and ordered to be recorded.
Recorded the first day of October 1759   Test: George Lee CCW

Page 250.
Settle to Gray Privy Examination
To William Berryman, John Monroe and James Blair, Gent., greeting. Whereas Francis Settle the County of Westmoreland and Sarah Settle his wife by their indenture of feoffment having date the 21st day of September 1759 conveyed unto George Gray of this County of Stafford in fee simple estate of 134 acres lying in the Parish of Washington and County of Westmoreland and whereas the said Sarah Settle to not conveniently travel to our court to make acknowledgment of the said conveyance, therefore we do give unto you power to receive the personal acknowledgment which she shall be willing to make. Witness: George Lee clerk of our said County Court the 26th day of August.

Westmoreland Sct. At a court held for the said county the 25th day of September 1759 this commission for the privy examination of Sarah Settle wife of Francis Settle for relinquishment of her right of dower and inheritance of in and to the lands conveyed to George Gray is ordered to be recorded.
Recorded the 2nd day of October 1759   Test: George Lee CCW

Page 251.
Sanford's Will
In the name of God Amen, I Richard Sanford, Sr. of Westmoreland county being weak and sick of body but of perfect sense and sound memory do make this my last will and testament.

I give and bequeath unto my loving wife Susannah Sanford all my whole estate of what kind soever during her widowhood.

Item I give and bequeath to my son Richard Sanford [missing] plantation whereon he now lives in Fairfax County containing [missing] Negroes; Cuffy and Moll and the said Moll's future increase.

Item I give and bequeath to my son Robert Sanford my two negroes; Jacob and Joan and the said Joan's future increase. Only my will and desire is that the first child that the said Joan brings and lives to be two years old do give to my granddaughter Susannah Sanford, daughter of my son Edward Sanford or 15 pounds current money.

Item I give and bequeath to my son Edward Sanford the plantation whereon I now live on in Westmoreland County containing two hundred acres. Also, two Negroes; Wepster and Judea and the said Judea's future increase.

Item I give and bequeath to my daughter Frances Harrison 15 pounds current money after my will is proved.

Item I lend to my daughter Elizabeth Cox, negro girl Jenny and her increase during her natural life and after her death return to my three sons.

Item I give and bequeath to my daughter Ann Muse 1,000 pounds crop tobacco to be paid after my will is proved.

Item I give and bequeath to my kinsman Augustine Sanford, one pistole to be paid to him by my executors after my will is proved.

Item it is my will and desire is that my three negroes; Congo Tom, Old Jenny and Little Tom shall be sold for money to discharge my just debts if my executor thinks fit, otherwise they paying the said debts may dispose of the negroes as they think proper.

Item I give and bequeath to my grand son Franklin Perry, 1 shilling sterling which I allot to be in full part of his mother Susannah Perry, deceased part of my whole estate.

Item I give and bequeath to my grand son Richard Muse 1 shilling which I allot to be in full part of his mother Mary Muse, deceased part of my whole estate.

Item I give and bequeath to my grand son Thomas Muse 1 shilling which I allot to be in full part of his mother Sarah Muse, deceased part of my whole estate.

Item all the rest of my estate herein [not other] wise bequeathed I give and bequeath to my three sons [xxx] equally between them.

Item lastly, I do appoint my three sons Richard Sanford, Robert Sanford and Edward Sanford whole and sole executors of this my last will and testament.

In confirmation whereof I have hereunto set my hand and affixed my seal this 25th day of July 1757

Signed Sealed and delivered in presence of   Richard Sanford
John Sanford
Augustine Sanford
Katherine Sanford

Westmoreland Sct. At a Court held for said County the 30th day of October 1759 last will and testament of Richard Sanford, deceased was presented into Court by the executors therein named who made oath thereto and being duly proved by the oath of all the witnesses thereto is admitted to record in upon the motion of the said executors and their performance what the law in such cases require certificate is granted them for obtaining a probate thereof in due form.

Recorded the second day of November 1759   Test: George Lee CCW

Page 253.

<u>Harding [Hardin] & Wife to Brown Indenture</u>

This indenture made this 29th day of October 1759 between Thomas Harding [Hardin] and Sarah Harding his wife of [missing] of the one part and John Brown of Westmoreland County, planter of the other part. Thomas Harding and Sarah Harding in consideration of two [missing] current money of Virginia has sold to John Brown a tract of land containing 50 acres situated in the Parish of Cople in County of Westmoreland containing 50 acres and bounded as followeth, vizt; beginning at a corner of a marked red oak tree which divides the land from the land formerly Daniel Hutt's, deceased and now in possession of Gerard Hutt and the land formerly Andrew Read's but now in the possession of Ruth Read the widow and relict of Coleman Read, deceased and the land that formerly belonged to Samuel Morris, from thence bounding North East on said road and extending South East 120 poles to a marked hickory corner tree standing on the south side of a swamp and in the line of the said road, from thence extending South East 68 poles to a marked red oak standing on the side of a hill and in line of the land that formerly belonged to Thomas Moberly, from thence bounding Southwest on said Moberly's and extending along the said Moberly's line North West 120 poles to a marked poplar corner tree the said Moberly's, from thence extending North East along the line of the said Hutt's 68 poles to the first beginning corner tree. In witness whereof the parties above mentioned have interchangeably set their hands and seals the day and year first mentioned.

Signed sealed and delivered in presence of   Thomas Harden [Hardin]
Vincent Lewis, Richard Beale   Sarah Harden (her mark)
Gerard Hutt

Westmoreland Sct. At a Court held for the said County the 30th day of October 1759 Thomas Harden and Sarah Harden his wife came into Court and personally acknowledged this deed of feoffment, together with the livery of seizen and receipt thereon endorsed passed from Thomas

Harden and Sarah Harden his wife to John Brown. Sarah Harden being first privily examined relinquished her right of dower to the same and ordered to be recorded.
Recorded the fifth day of November 1759   Test: George Lee CCW

Page 256.
Price to Wheeler Lease
This indenture made 21st day of September 1759 between Thomas Price of the Parish of St. Paul's and county of Stafford, planter of the one part and William Wheeler and Ann Wheeler his wife of Westmoreland, planter of the other part. Witnesseth that Thomas Price in consideration of the annual rents of three pounds current money of Virginia and the quitrents of 100 acres of land has let and to farm let that tenement of land in Westmoreland and bounded as followeth: Beginning on the south side of the main branch of Roziers Creek and at the upper side of Thomas Chancellor's land running thence up the said run westerly to Thomas Peach beginning tree thence southerly along a line of marked trees which divides this land and the land of Thomas Peach to a large road thence easterly, down the said road to Thomas Chancellor's line, thence westerly along Chancellor's line to the first beginning; the said bounded land being a plantation whereon Thomas Price, father to the said Thomas Price formerly lived. To have and to hold the land from the day of the date hereof for and during the life of William Wheeler and Ann Wheeler her life and should they have children for their lives. If they have no child, then after their decease for John Morgan's his life yielding and paying the aforesaid annual rents yearly on the 25th day of December. In witness whereof the parties aforesaid have, either to other, at these presents, interchangeably set their hands and seals the day month and year first mentioned.

Signed Sealed and delivered in presence of   Thomas Price
Calvert Jones   William Wheeler
David Jones
Samuel Meakey (his mark)

Westmoreland Sct. At a court held for the said county the 30th day of October 1759 this Thomas Price came into court and personally acknowledged this lease of land by him passed to William Wheeler to be his proper act and deed and ordered to be recorded.
Recorded the 9th day of November 1759   Test: George Lee CCW

Page 258.
Martin & Wife to Berryman Indenture
This Indenture made the 15th day of July 1759 between John Martin and Mary Ann Martin his wife of the Parish of Washington and County of Westmoreland of the one part and James Berryman of the parish and county aforesaid of the other part. Witnesseth that the said John Martin in consideration of 46 pounds current money of Virginia has sold unto James Berryman two tracts of land containing by estimation 600 acres situate and being on the head of Weedon's Dam in Westmoreland County, part of the land formerly purchased of John Triplett of King George County and the other part from the executors of George Blackmore by Francis Settle and by Francis Settle and Sarah Settle his wife to me the aforesaid John Martin by deed dated the 11th day of November 1755. In witness whereof the said John Martin and Mary Ann Martin have heretunto set their hands and seals the day and year first mentioned.

Signed Sealed and delivered in the presence of   John Martin
Samuel Love   Mary Ann Martin
[xxxx]

Be it remembered that on the date of the within full and peaceable possession and seizen of the lands and premises within mentioned was given and delivered by the within named John Martin to the within named James Berryman by turf and twigg part of the premises to hold to him the said James Berryman and his heirs to the uses within mentioned.
In the presence of
John Hilton
Christopher Mothershead

Received of the within named James Berryman, the within mentioned sum of 46 pounds current money of Virginia it being the consideration mentioned in the within deed, received the 15th day of

July 1759. John Martin
John Hilton
Christopher Mothershead
Westmoreland Sct. At a court held for the said county the 27th day of November 1759 John Martin, Gent., came into court and personally acknowledged together with the livery of seizen and the receipt thereon endorsed this deed for land by him passed to James Berryman to be his proper act and deed and ordered to be recorded
Recorded the 12th day of December   Test: George Lee CCW

Page 260.

Brown's Will

In the name of God Amen, August the 11th, 1759. I William Brown of Parish of Washington and County of Westmoreland, planter being very infirm in body but of perfect mind and memory to make and ordain this my last will and testament.

Imprimis, I give my land unto my son William Brown and to the male heirs of his body and for want of such heirs I give my land unto my son John Brown and to the male heirs of his body.

Item I likewise give unto my son William Brown, negroes; Joe, Young Coffee and Benn; also my young horse, great chest.

Item I give unto my son John Brown negroes; John, Old Coffee, Dick and Aaron; my great trunk, also my mare and colt and spoon moulds. Also, my new case.

Item I give unto my daughter Mary Hore Negroes; Tom, Willy and Will.

Item I given to my daughter Jane Price Negroes; James and George.

Item I given to my daughter Elizabeth Craighill Negroes; Jude and her young child. My best bed, bolster rug with two pair sheets, bedstead, and cord. Also, an iron griddle and my new desk.

Item I give unto my daughter Margaret Williams Negroes; Young Sarah and her child. My second-best bed with furniture. Also, one cow and calf.

Item I given to my daughter Hannah Butler Negroes; Lettice and Old Sarah. My next best bed with furniture, one cow and calf, the new bed tick now made in the house, 10 yards of sheeting linen.

Item I give my sheep to be divided between my daughters Jane Price, Elizabeth Craighill and Hannah Butler

Item I give to my daughter Anna Brown my old desk.

Item I give to my son William Brown my copper kettle.

Item it is my desire that the cotton, linen and hone I have now by me be for the use of my people above mentioned.

Item my other estate not mentioned here my desire is to be sold by my executors and the money arising from thence to be equally divided between my above-mentioned children.

Item the money now in hand of Mr. Johnson in the sterling money due from the said Johnson, my desire is my son William Brown to collect the same in the said money and goods arising from the sterling be equally distributed between my aforesaid children.

Item my desire is that my son William Brown take into his care my crop now on the ground and to be sold by him to the best advantage in the money on the goods from thence arising to be equally divided among my children. My son William Brown to be allowed 5 pounds the said crop for his trouble.

Item my will and desire that my estate be not inventoried, nor appraised but divided according to this my last will and testament.

Item I do appoint my loving sons William Brown and John Brown executors to this my last will and testament.

In witness whereof I have hereunto set my hand and seal the day and year above written

Signed sealed and delivered in the presence of us   William Browne
Francis Williams, Anthony Paton [Peyton]
John Paton [Peyton

Westmoreland Sct. At a court held for the said County this 30th day of October 1759 this last Will and Testament of William Brown deceased was presented in court by William Brown his son one of the executors therein named and being proved by the oath of Anthony Peyton one of the witnesses thereto is ordered to be lodged for further proof

Westmoreland Sct. At a court held for the said County the 27th day of November 1759 this last Will and Testament of William Brown deceased was again presented into Court by William Brown [one of his executors] who made oath [missing] and being fully proved by the oath of Francis Williams and John Peyton witnesses thereto was ordered to be recorded and upon motion of the said executor and his performing what the law such cases require, certificate is granted him for obtaining a probate thereof in due form.
Recorded the 12th day of December 1759   Test: George Lee CCW

Page 263.
Chandler's Will
In the name of God Amen, I Joseph Chandler of the Parish of Cople and County of Westmoreland, Planter's will and in health of body and of sound mind and memory do make this my last will in manner and form following.
Item I give and bequeath to my son Thomas Chandler and his heirs forever five Negroes; Frank, Betty, Letty, Tom and Isaac. In one third part of my personal estate which estate is to be paid him at the age of 21 years and he is to be educated and maintained out of his said estate [until he] arrives to the age of 18 years at which time [he is to] act in due for himself but not to receive estate or have any education or maintenance out of it until he arrives at his lawful age.
Item I give and bequeath to my daughter Elizabeth Chandler and her heirs forever Negro George and one third part of my personal estate.
Item I give and bequeath to my daughter Mary Chandler and her heirs forever Negro Will and one third part of my personal estate.
Item I give and bequeath to my wife Frances Chandler during her widowhood a maintenance out of my estate suitable to her station in full of her dower.
Item it is my will and desire that my estate be kept together until my eldest daughter arrives at the age of 21 years or day of marriage which shall first happen and then my personal estate to be equally divided among my children and it is my further desire that my children and particularly be educated and maintained suitable to his estate.
Lastly, I constitute and appoint my friend Richard Lee, Esq. executor and my wife Frances Chandler executrix of this my last will and testament as well as both to be guardians to my children.
In witness whereof I have hereunto set my hand and seal the 17th day of March 1758.
Signed sealed published and delivered in the presence of us   Joseph Chandler
Joseph Lane, Mary Luck [her mark]
Thomas Hughes, Ambrose Lipscomb
Codicil to the above will
I will and bequeath to my [missing] ann Chandler, Negro Betty's child Jenny with her increase to her in her heirs forever. Witness my hand and seals this 19th day of April 1759
Signed sealed and published before   Joseph Chandler (his mark)
Joseph Lane
Westmoreland Sct. At a court held for said County the 29th day of January 1760 this last will and testament of Joseph Chandler, deceased was presented into Court by Frances Chandler his relict who made oath thereto and the said will and codicil thereunder written being both proved by the oath of Joseph Lane a witness thereto was admitted to record and the said Frances Chandler in open court referring to stand to the said will relinquished all her right that she may claim by the aforesaid will and on motion of the said Frances Chandler and her performing what the law in such cases require certificate is granted her for obtaining a probate thereof in due form
recorded the 30th day of January 1760   Test: George Lee CCW

Page 265.
Corbin's Will
In the name of God Amen Gawin Corbin in the Parish of Cople and County of Westmoreland being weak of body but of sound sense and memory do this 29th day of October 17[xx] publish this my last will and testament in manner following.
Item I lend all my estate both real and personal to my dear wife during her widowhood and continuance in the county allowing my daughter Martha Corbin out of my estate a genteel

education and maintenance to the discretion of my executors; but if my wife continues a widow until my daughter Martha Corbin marries or comes to age of 21 years then it is my will and desire that my daughter shall have one half of my whole estate that my wife marries again or leaves the County then in that case my will and desire is that my wife shall be deprived of the request already made her and in lieu thereof shall only have one third of my estate real personal and the remaining two thirds of my estate shall immediately pass to my said daughter Martha Corbin and the heirs of her body. And in default of such heirs, I give one half of my estate unto my brother Richard Corbin's two youngest sons and to their heirs forever and the other half of my estate to the two youngest sons of my dear sister Tucker. If it should so happen that she is more than two sons but if not then I would have this half of my estate descend to her youngest son and heirs or their heirs forever.

Item my will and desire is that at the death of my dear wife that my whole estate both real and personal then in her possession descend to my daughter Martha Corbin and the heirs of her body lawfully begotten forever and for want of such heirs then to descend to the youngest sons of my brother Richard Corbin and [my] sister Tucker in manner as before mentioned

Item I give £20, to be sent for in course goods to the room of the Parish of Cople [for the use of] such who have many children and use their utmost endeavors to support them by honest labor and industry still find themselves from their numerous family incapable, and this bequest I will have distributed at the discretion of my executors.

Item it is my express desire that my daughter Martha Corbin do not marry until she arrives at the age of 21 years and then not without the consent of her guardians or the majority of them which if she does I desire my estate may be immediately descend to the youngest son of my brother Richard Corbin and my sister Tucker as I have before directed and my daughter Martha Corbin to have but one shilling my estate; this I desire that a prudent choice may be made of a man of tenor and family and that she may live happily in a matrimonial state.

Item I desire all my just debts they be paid as soon as possible

Item my will and desire is that godson Thomas Lee, son of Richard Henry Lee may be paid £150 to be applied to accomplishing his education when he is sent home.

Item my will is further that of my crops should not be sufficient to pay my debts that I would have my Caroline [county] lands sold to pay them, and it is my express desire that Edy, Truelove and Cyrus, three of my Negroes be sent to the West Indies and sold, and the money arising from the sale of them be applied to the paying of my debts.

Item I do hereby appoint my wife, Col. Richard Henry Lee, Thomas Ludwell Lee, Francis Lightfoot Lee and Richard Corbin executors of my will and guardians of my daughter Martha Corbin.

Item I give all my brothers and sisters nephews and nieces a mourning ring a piece of a guinea value.

Item it is my desire that my brother Richard Henry Lee may be one of my acting the executors.

Item my will and desire is that my estate may not be appraised as it may be attended with useless and unnecessary expense, trouble and confusion.

Signed sealed published before us   Gawen Corbin
Richard Henry Lee,
Richard Lingan Hall
Mary Allen
Mary Luck

Westmoreland Sct. At a court held for said County the 29th day of January 1760 this last will and testament of Gawen Corbin, Esq. was presented into Court by Mrs. Hannah Corbin and Richard Henry Lee, Esq. two of the executors therein named and made oath thereto and being proved by the oath of Richard Lingan Hall and Mary Allen two of the witnesses thereto is admitted to record and upon motion of the said executors and their performing what is usual in such cases, certificate is granted them for obtaining a probate thereof in due form.

Recorded the first day of February 1760   Test: George Lee CCW

Page 267.
<u>Spence to Sanford Indenture</u>
This Indenture made the 26th day of February 1760 between Patrick Spence of the Parish of Cople in the County of Westmoreland of the one part and Augustine Sanford of the aforesaid parish and

county of the other part. Witnesseth that the said Patrick Spence in consideration of the sum of 800 pounds of tobacco has sold to Augustine Sanford a dividend of 20 acres in the Parish of Cople and County of Westmoreland and bounded on the land of Augustine Sanford to the main run, so down the main run to the mouth of a branch thence up the said branch as far as where the land of the said Spencer begins, on the other side of the said branch which said water courses divide the said parcel of land from the other tract of Patrick Spence. In witness whereof the parties to these presents have hereunto set their hands and seals the day and year first mentioned.

Signed sealed and delivered in the presence of us   Patrick Spence
Robert Douglass
William Marmaduke
Francis Randall

Westmoreland Sct. At a court held for the said county the 26th day of February 1760 Patrick Spence came into court and personally acknowledged together with the livery of seizen and receipt thereon endorsed, this deed of feoffment by him passed to Augustine Sanford to be his proper act and deed and ordered to be recorded

Recorded this 3rd day of February 1760   John Lee, Jr. CCW

Page 270.
Berryman to Berryman Indenture
This indenture made the 21st day of November 1759 between Elizabeth Berryman of the County of Westmoreland and Parish of Washington of one part and William Berryman of the same parish and county of the other part. Witness that in consideration of 5 shillings and divers good causes me thereunto moving but more especially for the great love and affection I have unto my son William Berryman and he has not had any profits and advantages from his father's estate more than four negroes to wit; an old man, his wife, a child and a boy which I gave him as a beginning as also the land left him by his father and some small matter of stock and household furniture after which two of my other sons dying before they came of age to that behoof of the estate was in my care and whereas chief part of the profits was put to my son James Berryman's use in building the mill and flood gates two or three times and two pair of mill stones, and building a large brick house, kitchen and other outhouses and 30 pounds which my son James Berryman had to pay Mr. Ashton the money he borrowed to buy Neale's land with; as also the land he bought of Welch as also 70 pounds sterling paid Capt. Anthony Thornton for land left him by his father and many other advantages and whereas Dorothy Spiller left to my son William Berryman a large legacy which has not been fully paid him as also one negro man given to my said son William Berryman by her sister Beheathland Berryman which said negro was in his fathers and my possession, about 15 years, and he has not as yet had any satisfaction for the labor of the said negro therefore to do my said son William Berryman justice with my other sons according to my husband's will impowers me which I have always endeavored to do them all, and whereas I bought a tract of land of Cossum Bennett lying and being in the county and parish aforesaid which will appear by deeds recorded in Westmoreland court. Now this indenture witnesseth that for the considerations above mentioned, I the said Elizabeth Berryman doth give grant bargain and sell unto my said son William Berryman, his heirs and assigns forever, all that tract or parcel of land I bought and Cossum Bennett lying in being in the said County as will appear by deeds recorded in Westmoreland County. In witness whereof I the said Elizabeth Berryman as subscribed my name and affixed my seal to this indenture the day and year above written, to wit on the 21st day of November 1759.

Signed sealed and delivered in presence of   Elizabeth Berryman (her mark)
Thomas Clark
William Kendall
Valentine Hudson (his mark)
Andrew Thompson (his mark)
William Potes
Thomas Arrowsmith
John Massey
Received of five shillings within mentioned   Elizabeth Berryman (her mark)
Test: Thomas Clark

William Kendall
Valentine Hudson (his mark)
Andrew Thompson (his mark)
George Johnston (his mark)
William Potes
Thomas Arrowsmith
John Massey
Westmoreland Sct. At a court held for said County the 25th day of March 1760 this deed indented for land together with the receipt thereon endorsed passed from Elizabeth Berryman to William Berryman was proved by the oath of Valentina Hudson, Thomas Arrowsmith and John Massey three of the witnesses thereto and ordered to be recorded
Recorded this 20th day of May 1760   Test: George Lee CCW

Page 274.
Ashton to Massey Indenture
This indenture made the 24th day of March 1760 between John Ashton of the County of Westmoreland of one part and John Massey of the same county of the other part. Witnessed that John Ashton in consideration of the sum of 60 pounds current money of Virginia has sold unto John Massey the tract of land lying in the Parish of Washington in County of Westmoreland containing by estimation 100 acres and bounded as follows, to wit; westerly by a tract of land belonging to John Ashton, southerly by the mill swamp, easterly by the land of John Weedon and northerly by the land of the said John Massey and Dishman now in possession of Harrison which said tract of land upon the death of Burditt Ashton without will descended to the said John Ashton party hereto in fee simple as his eldest son and heir at law. In witness whereof the said John Ashton have hereunto set his hand and seal the day and year aforesaid.
Signed sealed and delivered in the presence of   John Ashton, Jr.
Samuel Smith
Thomas Arrowsmith
Valentine Hudson (his mark)
Westmoreland Sct. At a court held for the said County the 25th day of March 1760 this deed of feoffment with the endorsements thereon passed from John Ashton to John Massey was proved by the oath of all the witnesses thereto and ordered to be recorded
recorded the 21st day of May 1760   Test: John Lee, Jr. CCW

Page 276-279.
Garner & Wife to Lee Indenture and Performance Bond
This indenture made the 9th day of January 1760 between Henry Garner of the Parish of Nottaway in the County of Amelia and Mary Garner his wife of the one part and George Lee of the Parish of Cople in the County of Westmoreland, Gent., of the other part. Witnesseth that Henry Garner and Mary Garner his wife in consideration of 80 pounds current money of Virginia has sold to George Lee a tract of land situated in the Parish of Cople and the County Westmoreland adjoining to the land of the said George Lee which tract was devised to the said Henry Garner by his father Henry Garner late of the parish and county last mentioned, deceased containing by estimation 115 acres. The parties to these presents have hereunto set their hands and seals the day and year first within written.
Sealed and delivered in the presence of us   Henry Garner
Richard Henry Lee   Mary Garner (her mark)
Willoughby Newton
Thomas Lawson
Bradley Garner
James Garner
Westmoreland Sct. At a Court held for the said County the 25th day of March 1760 this deed of feoffment together with the endorsements thereon pass from Henry Garner and Mary Garner his wife to George Lee, Gent., was proved by the oath of Richard Henry Lee, Bradley Garner and James Garner three of the witnesses thereto and ordered to be recorded.

Recorded the 21st day of May 1760   Test: John Lee, Jr. CCW

Page 279.
Garner & Wife to Lee Privy Examination
To Willoughby Newton, Richard Henry Lee and John Newton of the County of Westmoreland, Gent., greeting. Whereas Henry Garner of the County of Amelia and Mary Garner his wife by indenture of feoffment conveyed unto George Lee, Gent., of Westmoreland aforesaid the fee simple estate of 115 acres of land lying in the Parish of Cople and County aforesaid and whereas Mary cannot conveniently travel to our court to make acknowledgment of the said conveyance. Therefore, we give unto you power to receive the acknowledgment the said Mary Garner shall be willing to make before you. Witness George Lee, clerk of our said county court the 10th day of January 1760.
Westmoreland Sct. By virtue of the within commission we have examined Mary Garner the wife of Henry Garner touching the willingness to convey to George Lee, Gent., the fee simple estate on 115 acres of land and the said Mary Garner acknowledged all her right and title to the said land of her own free will and further she was willing to the deed of feoffment pass from her husband and herself should be recorded in Westmoreland court. Given under our hands and seals this 10th day of January 1760.
Willoughby Newton
Richard Henry Lee
Westmoreland Sct. At a Court held for the said County the 25th day of March 1760 this commission for the privy examination of Mary Garner for relinquishing her right of dower and thirds of in and to land sold by the said Henry Garner her husband George Lee being returned that she was there to consenting was ordered to be recorded
recorded the 21st day [missing]   Test: John Lee, Jr. CCW

Page 281-287
Turberville & Wife to Tidwell Indenture and Bond
Indenture made the 18th day of April 1760 between John Turberville of the Parish of Cople in County of Westmoreland, Gent., and Martha Turberville his wife of the one part and William Carr Tidwell of the same parish and county, planter of the other part. Witnessed that John Turberville and Martha Turberville his wife in consideration of 50 pounds current money of Virginia have sold unto William Carr Tidwell dividend of a tract of land lying in the Parish of Cople and County of Westmoreland commonly called and known by the name of "Narrows Point" [aka Hollowing Poynt Neck] on the upper side of Lower Machodoc River where the ship "Catherine" lies sunk, containing by estimation 140 acres. Bounded as followeth; beginning at the head of a Creek which divideth this land and the land formerly belonging to Capt. Thomas Youell and extending east southeast 160 poles to Lower Machodoc River thence southerly 200 poles along the said River to a small creek that divided this land and the land formerly belonging to Isaac Allerton, Esq., deceased and West Northerly along the land of the said Isaac Allerton to the first beginning. Which said land was first granted George Watts by patent bearing date the 20th day of July 1661 and after his decease the land descended by inheritance to William Watts his son and sole heir who by John Sturman his attorney duly and legally authorized thereto sold and conveyed the same to Abraham Smith of the said Parish of Cople in County of Westmoreland by deeds of lease and release bearing date the 23rd day of June 1691 and the said Abraham Smith sold and conveyed the said tract of land to James Lawhon by deed of feoffment bearing date the ninth day of June 1696 and the said James Lawhon sold and conveyed the said land to Abraham Field of the Parish of Washington in the County aforesaid who died possessed thereof without conveying or any way disposing of the same. Whereupon it became the proper inheritance of his daughters as co-heirs who by deed of gift bearing date the sixth day of September 1710 made over and conveyed the said land to their brother in law David Rozier, Jr., who by deeds of feoffment, bearing date the 25th day of July 1721 made over the land to Frances Asbury [Francis Awbrey] who by deed of feoffment bearing date the 31st day of August 1726 conveyed and made over the land to Major George Turberville who by his last will and testament bearing date the 16th day of October 1740 did give and devise the said land to the said John Turberville, party to these presents. In witness whereof the parties first above

named to these present indentures have interchangeably set their hands and seals they in the year first above written
sealed and delivered in the presence of us   John Turberville
Joseph Lane   Martha Turberville
William Rochester
George Turberville
Westmoreland Sct. At a Court held for the said County the 29th day of April 1760 John Turberville personally acknowledged together with the endorsements thereon this deed of feoffment by him passed to William Carr Tidwell and ordered to be recorded
recorded the 21st day of May 1760   Test: John Lee, Jr. CCW

Page 287
Turberville & Wife to Tidwell Privy Examination
To, Richard Henry Lee, John Newton and Richard Jackson, Gent., greeting. Whereas John Turberville of the County of Westmoreland and Martha Turberville his wife by their indenture of feoffment bearing date the 18th day of April 1760 conveyed unto William Carr Tidwell of the County aforesaid the fee simple estate of 140 acres of land lying in the Parish of Cople in County aforesaid and whereas the said Martha Turberville cannot conveniently travel to record to acknowledged the conveyance. Therefore, we give unto you the power to receive her personal acknowledgment of the said Martha Turberville shall be willing to make. Witness George Lee, clerk of our said County court the 28th day of April 1760.
By virtue of a commission to was bearing date the 28th day of April 1760 we have examined Martha Turberville the wife of John Turberville privily and apart from her husband and she declared that she is willing that the said land should be recorded in Westmoreland County and she freely relinquished her right of dower to the same. Given under our hands and seals of the County aforesaid this 29th day of April 1760
Willoughby Newton
Richard Jackson
Westmoreland Sct. Is a Court held for the said County the 29th day of April 1760 this commission for the privy examination of Martha Turberville wife of John Turberville, Gent., Or relinquishing her right of dower and thirds of in and to land sold by her said to William Carr Tidwell being returned executed was ordered to be recorded.
Recorded the 23rd day of May 1760   Test: John Lee, Jr. CCW

Page 289.
Spillman's Will
This last will and testament William Spillman being in perfect sense and memory though weak.
Imprimis, I give to my youngest daughter Margaret Spillman, one bed and furniture and one cow and calf and 10 shillings worth in pewter.
Item I give to my daughter Lettice Dulin one cow and calf.
I make my loving sons Thomas Spillman, William Spillman and John Spillman my whole executors and my land and improvements to be equally to be divided between the three brothers, my beloved sons, this being my last will and testament. As witness whereof thereunto set my hand and fixed my seal.   William Spillman (his mark)
Robert Frank
William Piper
Peter Jett
Westmoreland Sct. At a court held for the said county the 29th day of April 1760 this last will and testament of William Spillman, deceased was presented into court by the executors therein named who made oath thereto and being proved by the oaths of William Piper and Peter Jett, two of the witnesses thereto is admitted to record, and on motion of the said executors and their performing what is usual certificate is granted for obtaining a probate thereof in due form.
Test: John Lee, Jr. CCW

Page 290.

Pope's Will

In the name of God Amen, I Humphrey Pope of the Parish of Washington and the County of Westmoreland being weak of body but of perfect sense and memory to make and ordain this my last will and testament.
I give my loving wife my land and all the rest of my estate that can be saved after my debts is paid for her life and after her death my desire is that my son John Pope may have my land and no more of my estate and that all the rest of my estate may be equally divided between my other four children, Humphrey Pope, Benjamin Pope, Mary Pope and Nathaniel Pope.
Lastly, I appoint my loving wife Sarah Pope my whole and sole executrix of this my last will and testament. In witness whereof I have hereunto set my hand and seal this 9th day of August 1759.
Signed Sealed and delivered in the presence of   Humphrey Pope
John Muse
Alvin Mothershead (his mark)
Joseph Eidsen
Westmoreland Sct. At a court held for the said county the 27th day of May 1760 this last will and testament of Humphrey Pope, deceased was presented into court and proved by the oaths of John Muse and Joseph Eidsen, two of the witnesses thereto and ordered to be recorded, and John Bayne suggesting to the court that Sarah Pope, relict and executrix of the said deceased refusing to take upon herself the burthen of the execution of the said will, on motion of the said John Bayne and his performing all such things as the law in such cases requires administration, with the will annexed of all and singular the goods & chattles of the said deceased is in due form granted him.
Recorded the 16th day of June 1760   Test: John Lee, Jr. CCW

Page 291.
Lamkin vs Rush Arbitration Bond

Know all men by these presents that I Peter Lamkin of the County of Westmoreland am held and firmly bound unto Vincent Rust of the same county in the penal sum of 500 pounds current money which payment well and truly to be made and done I bind myself firmly by these presents. Sealed with my seal and dated this 22nd day April 1760.
The condition of the above obligation is such that whereas a dispute has arisen between Peter Lamkin and Vincent Rust concerning the settling of the bounds of their land, and the parties have mutually agreed to leave the matter in dispute to William Garland to determine the same and return thereof to each party and to stand to his settlement then the obligation to be void and of no effect otherwise to stand in full force, power and virtue.
Test   Peter Lamkin
Francis G[ilbert]

Page 292.
Lamkin vs Rush Arbitration Report & Award

This is to certify that I met on the land of disputed between Mr. Vincent Rust and Mr. Peter Lamkin and began at a white oak stump marked as a corner standing near the fork of a branch being the head corner of William Smith's patent, thence run northeast to the number of poles mentioned in the patent to a stake standing near two large red oaks, thence run South 48° East along a new marked line of trees to a corner hickory standing on the head of Yeocomico River.
24th May 1760   William Garland
Westmoreland Sct. At a court held for the said county the 24th day of May 1760 this bond together with the arbitrator's report from Peter Lamkin to Vincent Rust was presented into court by the said Rust and ordered to be recorded.
Recorded 18th day of June 1760   Test: John Lee, Jr. CCW

Page 292.
Rust vs Lamkin Arbitration Bond

Know all men by these presents that I Vincent Rust of the County of Westmoreland am held and firmly bound unto Peter Lamkin of the same county in the penal sum of 500 pounds current money which payment well and truly to be made and done I bind myself firmly by these presents. Sealed

with my seal and dated this 23rd day April 1760.
The condition of the above obligation is such that whereas a dispute has arisen between Vincent Rust and Peter Lamkin concerning the settling of the bounds of their land, and the parties have mutually agreed to leave the matter in dispute to William Garland to determine the same and return thereof to each party and to stand to his settlement then the obligation to be void and of no effect otherwise to stand in full force, power and virtue.

Test   Vincent Rust
Francis Gilbert
William Garland

Page 293.
Rust vs Lamkin Arbitration Report & Award
This is to certify that I met on the land of disputed between Mr. Vincent Rust and Mr. Peter Lamkin and began at a white oak stump marked as a corner standing near the fork of a branch being the head corner of William Smith's patent, thence run northeast to the number of poles mentioned in the Patent to a stake standing near two large red oaks, thence run South 48° East along a new marked line of trees to a corner hickory standing on the head of Yeocomico River.
24th May 1760   William Garland
Westmoreland Sct. At a court held for the said county the 24th day of May 1760 this bond together with the arbitrator's report passed from Vincent Rust to Peter Lamkin was presented into court by the said Lamkin and ordered to be recorded.
Recorded 18th day of June 1760   Test: John Lee, Jr. CCW

Page 293.
Edwards to Grigsby Lease
This indenture made the 20th day of April 1760 between Benjamin Edwards of county of Loudoun and parish of [missing], ordinary keeper and Jane Edwards his wife of the one part and Aaron Grigsby of the Parish of Brunswick and county of King George, planter of the other part. Witnesseth that Benjamin Edwards and Jane Edwards his wife in consideration of 5 shillings sterling has sold unto Aaron Grigsby a parcel of land lying in the Parish of Washington and County of Westmoreland containing by estimation 100 acres. Bounded as followeth; Joining upon Mr. Samuel Thornbury, Mr John Thornbury, Mr. Francis Balthrop, deceased and others and being part of a patent granted to Mr. Robert Alexander, deceased. To have and to hold from the day of the date hereof for and during the term of one year from thence next ensuing yielding and paying the rent of one ear of Indian corn on the birthday of our Lord God if demanded. To the extent that by virtue for transferring uses into possession the said Aaron Grigsby may be in the actual possession of the premises and be thereby enabled to take and accept of a grant and release of the reversion and inheritance thereof to him and his heirs forever. In witness whereof the said Benjamin Edwards hath hereunto set his hand and seal the day month and year first above written
Signed sealed and delivered in the presence of us   Benjamin Edwards
Calvert Jones
David Jones
Robert Monday (his mark)
Westmoreland Sct. At a court held for the said county the 24th day of June 1760 this lease of land passed from Benjamin Edwards to Aaron Grigsby was proved by the oaths of all the witnesses thereto and ordered to be recorded.
Recorded the 1st day of July 1760   Test: John Lee, Jr. CCW

Page 295.
Edwards to Grigsby Release
This indenture made the 21th day of April 1760 between Benjamin Edwards of county of Loudoun, ordinary keeper and Jane Edwards his wife of the one part and Aaron Grigsby of the Parish of Brunswick and county of King George, planter of the other part. Witnesseth that Benjamin Edwards in consideration of 100 pounds current money of Virginia has sold and released unto Aaron Grigsby a parcel of land lying in the Parish of Washington and County of Westmoreland containing by

Westmoreland County, Virginia Deeds & Wills DB13, 1756-1761

estimation 100 acres in his actual possession now being by virtue of a bargain and sale made by Benjamin Edwards bearing date the day next before the day of the date hereof and by force of the statute of transferring uses into possession a parcel of land lying in the Parish of Washington and County of Westmoreland containing by estimation 100 acres bounded as followeth; Joining upon Mr. Samuel Thornbury, Mr John Thornbury, Mr. Francis Balthrop, deceased and others and being part of a patent granted to Mr. Robert Alexander, deceased. In witness whereof the said Benjamin Edwards hath hereunto set his hand and seal the day month and year first above written
Signed sealed and delivered in the presence of us   Benjamin Edwards
Calvert Jones
David Jones
Robert Monday (his mark)
Westmoreland Sct. At a court held for the said county the 24th day of June 1760 this release of land indented passed from Benjamin Edwards to Aaron Grigsby was proved by the oaths of all the witnesses thereto and ordered to be recorded.
Recorded the 2nd day of July 1760   Test: John Lee, Jr. CCW

Page 298.
Settle to Gray Indenture
This indenture made the 26th day of March 1759 between Francis Settle and Sarah Settle his wife of the Parish of Washington and County of Westmoreland of the one part and George Gray of Stafford County of the other part. Witnesseth that Francis Settle, blacksmith and Sarah Settle his wife for a good and valuable consideration of the sum of 96 pounds current money of Virginia has sold unto George Gray a tract of land containing 135 acres lying in the County of Westmoreland and bounded as followeth; beginning near Washington's Mill in the line of Thomas Chancellor at the main road that leads to the Round Hill Church running up the said road 280 poles to the Round Hill Church yard, thence the head of the spring branch down the said branch to Bernard's line, thence southerly along Bernard's line to the main county road thence down the said county road to Thomas Chancellor's corner tree, thence along Chancellor's line to the beginning containing 135 acres and being part of tract formerly taken up and patented by Francis Gray, great grandfather to the said George Gray and the other part of the said parcel patented by Nathaniel Gray, father to the said George Gray which said tract of land patented by Francis Gray the elder has had the entail broken by twelve good and lawful free holders of said County of Westmoreland. In witness whereof the said Francis Settle and Sarah Settle his wife have hereunto set their hands and seals the day and year above written.
Signed Seale and delivered in the presence of   Francis Settle
Nathaniel Gray   Sarah Settle (her mark)
William Canfield (his mark)
William Berryman
James Blair
Westmoreland Sct. At a court held for the said county the 25th day of Sept 1759 this deed of feoffment passed from Francis Settle and Sarah Settle his wife to George Gray by the oaths of Nathaniel Gray and Samuel Blair two of the witnesses thereto and ordered to be lodged for further proof.   Test: John Lee, Jr. CCW
Westmoreland Sct. At a court held for the said county the 29th day of July 1760 this deed of feoffment together with the endorsements thereon was this day fully proved by the oath of William Berryman a witness thereto and ordered to be recorded
Recorded the 6th day of August 1760   .   Test: John Lee, Jr. CCW
[Ed White note: Entail normally was to heirs of his/her body. "Broken" means that by court action the entail was abolished, allowing a sale by someone out of the entail chain]

Page 307.
Lane's Will
In the name of God Amen, the 19th day of August 1758, I William Lane of Cople Parish in the County of Westmoreland being sick in body but of good and sound memory do make, constitute, ordain, and declare this my last will and testament in manner form following.

Item I give and bequeath unto my son James Lane by land and plantation whereon I now live to him and his heirs forever.

Item I give and bequeath unto my said son James Lane one half of the land that I bought of being and lying in Fairfax County to him and his heirs forever.

Item I give and bequeath to my son William Carr Lane my tract of land that I bought of Elizabeth Bailey and her son William Bailey to him and his heirs forever

Item I give unto my son Joseph Lane my land and plantation I bought of William Walker and the other half the land the has not been bequeath already that I bought of William Eskridge to him and his heirs forever lawfully begotten of his body and in default of such heirs to fall to my son William Carr Lane and his heirs forever.

Item I give and bequeath unto my son James Lane one Negro man named Scissis which he has now in his possession and one Negro boy named Sam to him and his heirs forever.

Item I give and bequeath to my daughter Hannah Middleton one Negro girl named Magg and her increase forever, and the Negro boy Sam which she has now in her possession to her at her heirs forever, in the cattle that I have already given her they and their increase to her and her heirs forever.

Item I give and bequeath unto my son William Carr Lane one Negro man named Toby and one Negro girl named Hannah that he has now in his possession and her increase to him and his heirs forever, and one Negro man named Dick to him and his heirs forever.

Item I give and bequeath unto My Son Joseph Lane, Negro Rose and her increase to him and his heirs forever, Negro boy Tom, Judah and her increase to him and his heirs forever, in Negro girl Prew and her increase to him and his heirs forever.

Item I give and bequeath unto My Son William Carr Lane, Negro Cate and her increase to him and his heirs forever.

Item I give and bequeath unto my loving wife Martha Lane during her life or widowhood all my whole estate and after her decease [my children] to receive their lands and legacies.

Item I give and bequeath unto my sons and daughters my whole estate it has not been bequeath already to be equally divided between James Lane, Hannah Middleton, William Carr Lane and Joseph Lane to them my children and their heirs forever after my loving wife's decease.

Item I do constitute and appoint My loving Wife Martha Lane, James Lane, William Carr Lane and Joseph Lane executrix and executors of this my last will and testament. As witness I have hereunto set my hand and seal

Signed sealed and delivered in the presence of   William Lane (his mark)
Letuice Gill (her mark)
Elizabeth Walker (her mark)
Daniel McKenny (his mark)

Westmoreland Sct. At a court held for the said County the 26th day of August 1760 this last will and testament by William Lane, Sr. deceased was presented into Court by William Carr Lane and Joseph Lane to of the executors therein named who made oath thereto and being proved by the oath of all the witnesses thereto was admitted to record, and upon motion of the said executors and their performance what is usual and such cases a certificate is granted them for obtaining a probate thereof in due form.

Recorded the ninth day of September 1760   Test: John Lee, Jr. CCW

Page 304.

Hall & Wife to Newbury & Courtney Assignment of Lease

We the within named Ashton Hall and Mary Hall his wife do assign and make over the within demised lease unto Robert Newbury and Samuel Courtney for and during our natural lives within mentioned, in consideration whereof the said Robert Newbury and Samuel Courtney is to pay to the said Ashton Hall 24 pounds current money on or before the 15th day of July 1760.

                     Ashton Hall
                     Mary Hall

NB. The within named James Courtney do agree to take the said Robert Newbury and Samuel Courtney for the within rents and clear the said Ashton Hall thereof.

George Rust   James Courtney

Presley Hall
Leasure Hall
Westmoreland Sct. At a court held for the said county the 28th day of October 1760, this assignment of lease from Ashton Hall and Mary Hall his wife to Robert Newbury and Samuel Courtney was proved by the oaths of George Rust and Presley Hall two of the witnesses thereto and ordered to be recorded.
Recorded the 7th day of November 1760   Test: John Lee, Jr. CCW

Page 304.
Wilkinson's Will
In the name of God Amen, I Tylor [Taylor/Tyler] Wilkinson [Wilkerson], the elder, of Westmoreland County being very sick and weak but in perfect sense and memory to ordain and appoint this to be my last will and testament in manner and form.
I give unto my well-beloved son, Tylor Wilkinson one cow and calf.
I give unto my sons William Wilkinson, James Wilkinson, Thomas Wilkinson, Garard Wilkinson and Robert Wilkinson and Elizabeth Roberts 1 shilling sterling apiece in full of my estate.
Item I leave the use of all the rest of my estate to my loving wife Elizabeth Wilkinson during her natural life, also my will is that after the death of my loving wife all the rest of my estate not above given be and remain to my beloved son John Wilkinson to him and his heirs forever be taking care of his mother.
Lastly, I appoint my loving wife and my beloved son John Wilkinson my whole and sole executors of this my last will and testament. As witness my hand and seal this sixth day of April 1758.
John Baley [Bailey]   Tyler Wilkinson (his mark)
George Wilkinson
Westmoreland Sct. At a court held for the said County the 28th day of October 1760 the last will and testament of Tyler Wilkinson was presented into Court by John Wilkinson one of the executors therein named who made oath thereto and being proved by the oath of both the witnesses thereto is admitted to record and on motion of the said executors and his performing what the law in such cases require certificate is granted him for obtaining a probate thereof in due form.
Recorded the seventh day of November 1760   Test: John Lee, Jr. CCW

Page 305.
Sanford's Will
In the name of God Amen, I Robert Sandford [Sanford] of the Parish of Cople in County of Westmoreland being very sick and weak of body but of perfect mind and sound memory do make and ordain this my last will and testament in manner and form following.
Item I do give and bequeath unto my son James Sanford three crop hogsheads of tobacco I have already inspected in Nominy Warehouse, allowing my tobacco debts first to be paid out of the same.
Item I given to my daughters Winifred Sanford one crop hogshead of tobacco which is also in Nominy Warehouse; and one choice cow
Item I do give unto my son Robert Sanford by large Bible; my Negro man Jack.
Item it is my will and desire that all my remaining estate besides what I have already given to be equally divided among my six children; John Sanford, Robert Sanford, James Sanford, Ann Moxley, Winifred Sanford and Jemima South.
Item it is my desire that the tobacco which I have before given unto my son James Sanford be sold for cash and delivered unto him at the age of 21 years.
Item I do constitute and appoint my son Robert Sanford my whole and sole executor of this my last will and testament. In witness whereof I have hereunto set my hand and affixed my seal this 22nd day of August 1760
Signed sealed and delivered in the presence of us   Robert Sanford (his mark)
Thomas Chilton, Jr.
Sarah Weaver (her mark)
Westmoreland Sct. At a court held for the said County the 28th day of October 1760 this last will and testament of Robert Sanford, deceased was presented into court by Robert Sanford the

executor therein named who made oath thereto and being proved by the oath of both the witnesses thereto is admitted to record on motion of the said executor and his performing what the law in such cases require certificate is granted him for obtaining a probate thereof in due form.
Recorded the fourth day of November [1760]   Test: John Lee, Jr. CCW

Page 307.
<u>Bushrod's Will</u>
In the name of God Amen, I John Bushrod of the Parish of Cople in the County of Westmoreland, Gent., Being sick and weak but of sound and disposing mind and memory do make and ordain this my last will and testament in manner and form following.
Imprimis I give and bequeath to my loving wife Mildred Bushrod and her heirs all and every the Negro slaves and all the stock I now hold and am possessed of or have any claim to by virtue of my intermarriage with her in the sum of 400 pounds current money of Virginia, the chariot I have sent for in Great Britain (when it arrives), and the two horses I designed for it, one large silver cup with two handles, one dozen silver spoons, which I have sent for in Great Britain (when they arrive), the bed and furniture, writing desk, covered armchair, dressing table and glass which is the furniture of my lodging chamber, as also the use of my waiting man Isaac for and during her natural life, the legacies aforesaid I design to be in full satisfaction of the dower of my said wife or any claim she may had to any part of my estate either real or personal and in case my will said wife shall not on the standing this devise, claim her dower of my estate after the decease, then the above bequest to be void.
Item I give and devise unto my granddaughter Mary Washington three Negroe slaves; Keren, Morly and Silly and their increase to be delivered to her when she arrives to the age of 18 years or marries which ever shall first happen. My daughter Hannah Washington to have the use and profits of the same till that time.
Item I give and devise unto my granddaughter Jeanny Washington three Negroe slaves; Phillis, Darkey and Nell and their increase to be delivered to her when she arrives to the age of 18 years or his married whichever shall first happen. My daughter Hannah Washington to have the use and profits of the same until that time.
Item I give and bequest all that tract of land whereon I now lives together with all the several tracts adjoining and also my water grist mill in the land thereto adjoining situate lying in being in the said Parish of Cople in County of Westmoreland and also the following 35 Negro slaves; Nero, Cate, Hannah, Sukey, Jemima, Billy, Pat, Abram, Kezia, Doz, Ralph, Abigal, Anthony, Dick, Violet, Clark, Joice, Harry, Alice, Jacob, Esaw, Peter, Boo, Tim, Willoughby, Baker, Isaac, Harvey, Phill, Daniel, Tom, Ben, Patience, Aaron and Daniel, and their increase. Also, my waiting man Isaac after the decease of my wife unto my daughter Hannah Washington and to her heirs and in default of such heirs male to the eldest daughter she shall have at the time of her death. In default of any heirs to my daughter Elizabeth Bushrod in the male heirs of her body.
Item I give and bequeath my land known by the name of "Forrest Land" lying in the parish aforesaid adjoining to the lands of Turberville and Cox and [missing] in the Parish of Washington and the County aforesaid adjoining Lee and McCarty's lands, and also 41 Negro slaves; George, Bridget, Betty, Mary, Jenny, Ned, Betty, Frank, Easter, Billy, Jeny, Frank, Winnie, Nan, Jimmy, Soloman, Adam, Charity, Nat, Abrabah, Jack, Sam, Dawson, Simon, Charlot, Sukey, Toney, Dinah, Betty, Peg, Moll, Isaac, Andrew, Nan, Mores, Bab, Beck, Will, Grace, and Judy, and their increase unto my daughter Elizabeth Bushrod and the heirs male of her body lawfully begotten and in default of such male heirs to the first daughter the said Elizabeth shall have. In default of any heirs to my daughter Hannah Washington in the male heirs of her body.
Item I give and bequeath to Lydia Bushrod Pettit, daughter of Mr. John Pettit in case her father spends all his estate and is unable to maintain her, the sum of £10 to be paid yearly for her maintenance out of the profits of my estate until she arrives at the age of 18 years or his married whichever shall first happen, exclusive of her board, provided that the said Lydia is permitted to live with my daughter Hannah Washington.
Item I give and bequeath unto my daughter Hannah Washington all my household furniture of what nature kind or quality so ever not before given as also all my stock of every kind and utensil belonging to the land and plantations I have herein before given her and one half of my horses.

I give and bequeath unto my daughter Elizabeth Bushrod all my stock of every kind and utensils belonging to the lands and plantations I have herein before given her as also all the residue of my personal estate.

Item I direct that my daughter Elizabeth Bushrod do live with her sister.

Item I confirm the gift of the eight following Negro slaves given to my daughter Hannah Washington; Cesar, Winah, Lucy, Jenny, Jeny, Joan and her two children; which was sundry goods and money that I have given to her since her marriage amounts to the full sum of what I promised with her intermarriage.

Item as I have devised several negroes of the same names to each of my daughters, to prevent any disputes I have given them with their mother's and the families together.

Item I constitute and appoint my friends Hon. Richard Corbin, Esq. and Major John Augustine Washington, executors of this my last will and testament. In witness whereof I have hereunto set my hand and seal the 14th day of February 1760.

signed declared and published in presence of   John Bushrod
William Booth
Sarah [xxx] (her mark)
Soloman [xxxx]

Westmoreland Sct. At a court held for the said County the 30th day of December 1760 this will of John Bushrod, Gent., deceased was presented into court and sworn to by John Augustine Washington one of the executors therein named, the same being proved by the oath of all the witnesses thereto subscribed, is admitted to record and upon motion of said executors in his performing what the law is such cases require certificate is granted him for obtaining a probate thereof in due form.

Recorded the 24th day of February 1761   Test: John Lee, Jr. CCW

Page 311-314.
Crabb & Wife to Partridge Lease & Performance Bond
This indenture made the 23rd day of September 1760 between Osmond Crabb and Jane Crabb his wife of Cople Parish in Westmoreland County of the one part and Matthew Partridge of the same parish and county of the other part. Witnessed that the said Osmond Crabb and Jane Crabb his wife in consideration of the rents and covenants herein after mentioned on the part of Matthew Partridge to be paid or performed hath demised and to farm let by these presents a tract of land containing 50 acres being the same more or less situate and lying in the Parish of Cople in County of Westmoreland it being part of the land that formerly belonged to John Footman, Gent., deceased and purchased by Mr. John Crabb, Jeremiah Carter which is bounded as follows; beginning at a red oak being a corner tree between Abraham Garner and John Crabb and running from thence in a straight line to another red oak in an old field belonging to the aforesaid John Crabb [missing] to the line between [missing] Hon. Robert Carter and the said John Footman, deceased. To have and to hold the tract of land during the lives of Osmond Crabb and Jane Crabb his wife or the longest lives of them yielding and paying yearly and every year during the term aforesaid on the 25th day of December, 950 pounds crop tobacco and cask and one shilling sterling for quick rents the first year only excepted which he is to have rent free in consideration whereof he is to build a dwelling house. In witness whereof the parties have hereunto set their hands and seals this day and year first above written.

Signed sealed and delivered in presence of us   Osmond Crabb
Abraham Garner   Jane Crabb
Joseph Garner
John Brown

Westmoreland Sct. At a court held for the said county the 31st day of March 1761 Osmond Crabb came into court and personally acknowledged this lease indented for land by him passed to Matthew Partridge in order to be recorded.

Recorded the 6th day of April 1761   Test: John Lee, Jr. CCW
[the Performance Bond was recorded at the same time]

Page 315.

Partridge's Will

In the name of God Amen, I Jane Partridge of the Parish of Cople in County of Westmorland being sick and weak of body but of good and perfect sense and memory do make and ordain this to be my last will and testament.

Imprimis; I give unto my son Peter Lamkin 5 shillings.
Item I given to my son [missing], warming pan.
Item I given to my son Ashton Lamkin 5 shillings.
Item give unto my daughter Eleanor Cox 5 shillings.
Item I given to my granddaughter Sarah Rust all my wearing apparel and my side saddle and bridle.
Item I given to my grandson Daniel Lamkin, one horse saddle and bridle.
Item I give unto my son Matthew Partridge three Negroes; Sarah, Winny and Sam and their increase. In 200 acres of land lying on Negro Run in Culpeper County together with all the rest of my estate both real and personal to him and his heirs forever.
In I do hereby constitute and appoint my son Matthew Partridge to be my whole and sole executor of this my last will and testament. In witness whereof I have hereunto set my hand and seal this 18th day of September 1760.

Sealed signed and declared in the presence of   Jane Partridge (her mark)
James Courtney
Samuel Rust

Westmoreland Sct. At a court held for the said County the 31st day of March 1761 the last will and testament of Jane Partridge, deceased was presented into Court by Matthew Partridge executor who made oath thereto and being proved by the oath of James Courtney and Samuel Rust two of the witnesses thereto admitted to record and upon motion of the said executor and his performing what the law is such cases require certificate is granted him for obtaining a probate thereof in due form.

Recorded the sixth day [missing]   George Lee: CCW

Page 316.
Rust to Wright Indenture

This indenture made the 29th day of January 1761 between John Rust, planter of Cople Parish in Westmoreland County of the one part and Francis Wright of the same Parish in County of the other part. Witnesseth that John Rust in consideration of 220 pounds current money of Virginia has sold by these presents to Francis Wright a tract of land which fell to me by devisee and the will of my grandfather John Rust containing 200 acres and bounded as followeth; beginning at the head of Peter Lamkin's Mill Pond which divides Northumberland County and Westmoreland County and adjoining the land of Robert Headley, deceased, and to the land of George Harrison and to the land of Parish Garner down to a branch which makes into the Tanyard Swamp and down said swamp to Peter Lamkin's Mill Pond and so continues along the said pond to the beginning. In witness whereof the parties to these presents have interchangeably set their hands and seals the day and year first within written.

Signed sealed and delivered in the presence of   John Rust
John Bailey
Daniel Bailey
George [Bannister]
[William] Cox

Memorandum; that on the 29th day of January 1761 John Rust and Ann Rust his wife made livery of seizen of the lands and appurtenances within mentioned by delivering turf and twigg and the ring of the door of the chief mansion house on the lands within mentioned unto the within named Francis Wright in the name of the whole land and appurtenances within granted bargained and sold according to the tenure form and effect of the within deed. In presence of
John Bailey
Daniel Bailey
George Bannister
William Cox

Westmoreland Sct. At a Court held for the said county the 31st day of March 1761 John Rust came into court and personally acknowledged, together with the livery of seizen and receipt thereon endorsed, this deed indented by him passed to Francis Wright to be his proper act and deed and ordered to be recorded.
Recorded the 7th day of April 1761   Test: George Lee CCW

Page 320.
Carter to Ransdell Lease
Indenture made the first day of January 1761 between Robert Carter of Westmoreland County and Virginia of one part and Edward Ransdell of the aforesaid County of the other part. Witnesseth that the said Robert Carter in consideration of the rents and covenants hereafter received on the part of Edward Ransdell has demised and to farm let by these presents 139 acres of land with appurtenances lying in the Parish of Cople and County of Westmoreland on the branches of Nominy River being part of a tract of land of 1000 acres and called "Brents Tract" and bounded as followeth; beginning at a stake near the road thence down the road to "B" another stake to the northward of the Spring Branch thence to "C" a fork of the said branch, thence down the Spring Branch to "D" the mouth thereof, thence up the West branch of Nominy River to "E" the last fork of the said branch, thence North 56° West to "H" a dead chestnut oak, thence to the beginning. To have and to hold the said land for and during the term of 21 years, yielding and paying yearly and every year from the date of these presents the sum of 6 pounds 15 shillings and 6 pence current of Virginia to the said Carter at his house in the city of Williamsburg. And the said Edward Ransdell does agree by these presents that he shall within three years after the date of these presents build on the said premises a house 32' x 20 and plant 50 apple trees and 50 peach trees and the same enclose with a lawful fence and from time to time and at all times during the said term well and sufficiently maintain and keep all and singular the massuages buildings and fences. In witness whereof the said Robert Carter and Edward Ransdell have hereunto interchangeably set their hands and seals the day and year first above written.

John Chilton   Robert Carter
John Redman   John Chilton
John S. Chilton

Westmoreland Sct. At a Court held for the said County the 21st day of March 1761 this lease for land indented passed from Robert Carter, Esq. to Edward Ransdell was proved by the oath of all witnesses thereto and ordered to be recorded.
Recorded the 8th day of April 1761   Test: George Lee CCW

Page 324.
Carter to Chilton Lease
This indenture made the first day of January 1761 between Robert Carter of Westmoreland County in Virginia of the one part and John Chilton of the same County of the other part. Witnesseth that the said Robert Carter in consideration of the rents and covenants hereafter received on the part of John Chilton has demised and to farm let by these presents 99 acres of land with appurtenances lying in the Parish of Cople and County of Westmoreland on the branches of Nominy River being part of a tract of land for 500 acres and called "Metcalf's Tract" and bounded as followeth; beginning at a small pine tree in a bottom, thence South 9° West 200 pole to a spanish oak on the north branch of Nominy River, thence down the said branch to Metcalf's beginning, thence North 182 poles to a stake, thence West by North to the beginning. To have and to hold the said land for and during the term of 21 years, yielding and paying yearly and every year from the date of these presents the sum of 5 pounds 1 shillings and 6 pence current of Virginia to the said Carter at his house in the city of Williamsburg. And the said Edward Ransdell does agree by these presents that he shall within three years after the date of these presents build on the said premises a house 16' x 20', a good common tobacco house and plant 50 apple trees and 50 peach trees and the same enclose with a lawful fence and from time to time and at all times during the said term well and sufficiently maintain and keep all and singular the massuages buildings and fences. In witness whereof the said Robert Carter and John Chilton have hereunto interchangeably set their hands and seals the day and year first above written.

Westmoreland County, Virginia Deeds & Wills DB13, 1756-1761

John Redman
John S. Chilton
Edward Ransdell
Robert Carter
John Chilton

Westmoreland Sct. At a Court held for the said County the 21st day of March 1761 this lease for land indented passed from Robert Carter, Esq. to John Chilton was proved by the oath of all witnesses thereto and ordered to be recorded.
Recorded the 8th day of April 1761

Test: George Lee CCW

Adams
  Robert, 73
Alexander
  Robert, 101
Allen
  Mary, 94
Allerton
  Ann, 61, 84
  Isaac, 19, 97
  Willoughby, 14, 37, 38, 61, 84
Allison
  Henry, 19
Anderson
  Walter, 6
Ariss
  John, 7
  Spencer, 19
Armistead
  John, 6
Arnold
  Weedon, 70
Arrowsmith
  Thomas, 95, 96
Asbury
  Henry, 40, 74, 87
  Mary, 40, 63
  Thomas, 63
Ashton
  Burditt, 55, 56, 65, 81, 96
  Charles, 55
  Henry, 8, 9, 23
  Jane, 9, 23
  John, 65, 81, 96
  Lawrence, 81
Atwell
  Elizabeth, 18
  Francis, 60
  Martha, 18
  Sarah, 19
  Thomas, 29
Awbrey
  Chandler, 18, 19
  Elizabeth, 18, 19
  Francis, 98
  James Sorrell, 18
Bailey
  Daniel, 108, 109
  Elizabeth, 103
  James, 31, 54, 77, 78, 84
  James, Jr., 77
  James, Sr., 77
  John, 10, 54, 58, 83, 84, 108, 109
  Stephen, 10, 77, 78
  William, 63, 103
Baker
  Anne, 24
  Butler, 21, 24, 25
  John, 24
  Susan, 21
Balfour
  James, 19, 64
Balthrop
  Francis, 101
  Virlinda, 20
Bankhead
  James, 21, 22, 53, 71
Bannister
  George, 109
Barnes, Mr., 29
Bayliss

Westmoreland County, Virginia Deeds & Wills: DB12, 1754-1756 and DB13, 1756-1761

Index

John, 16
Bayne
  Eleanor, 5
  John, 16, 17, 31, 32, 34, 35, 99
  Matthew, 5, 6, 8, 28, 29, 30, 32, 35, 49
  Richard, 17, 34
Beard
  George, 67
  John, 32, 33, 60, 67
Bennett
  Charles, 72
  Cossum, 95
  Daniel, 72
  Elizabeth, 17, 18, 72
  Solomon, 72
  Thomas, 17, 18, 63, 72, 84
  Thomas, Jr., 12, 23
  William, 72
Bernard
  Elizabeth, 49, 50
  Richard, 5, 49, 50
  William, 9, 42, 43, 44, 45, 46, 49, 50, 53, 62, 63, 65, 72, 80, 81, 86
Berryman
  Elizabeth, 95
  James, 20, 23, 27, 28, 33, 90, 91, 95
  William, 42, 43, 56, 62, 63, 79, 80, 81, 87, 95, 102
Black
  William, 48
Blackmore
  George, 9, 90
Blagg
  Abraham, 67, 85
Blair
  James, 5, 27, 33, 42, 43, 56, 58, 60, 61, 62, 63, 79, 80, 81, 87, 102
Blundell
  Thomas, 41, 74
Booth
  William, 107
Bowcock
  Thomas, 81
Bowe

William, 52
Brahan
  John, 49
Bridges
  William, 17, 34, 71
Broadhurst
  Elizabeth, 82
Brown
  Anna, 91
  Barbara, 38
  Charles, 31
  Elizabeth, 67
  George, 35
  James, 56, 68
  John, 11, 31, 38, 39, 54, 65, 82, 89, 91, 92, 107
  Manley, 31, 39
  Mary, 26, 38
  Original, 66, 67
  Richard, 31
  William, 91, 92
  William, Jr., 81
Bruer
  William, 55
Bryan
  Henry, 32
Bryant
  John, 52
  William, 52
Buckley
  William, 54
Bulger
  John, 12, 29, 50
Bushrod
  Elizabeth, 106
  John, 7, 13, 29, 30, 42, 43, 44, 46, 47, 105, 107
  Mildred, 105
Butler
  Anne, Jr., 27
  Christopher, 49
  Elizabeth, 27
  Hannah, 91
  Isabel, 34

James, 34
John, 27, 34, 72
Lawrence, 8, 27, 28, 30, 49
Nathaniel, 32, 35
Thomas, 9, 11, 27, 33, 34, 53
Thomas, Jr., 10, 27
Thomas, Sr., 10, 11
William, 34
Caddeen
  Hannah, 57
  John, 57
  Richard, 57
Callis
  Francis, 60
  Francis], 15
  Garland, 60
  Mary, 60
  Richard, 60
  William, 31, 59, 60
  William Overton, 60
Calvert
  George, 68, 69
Campbell
  Archibald, 25, 79
Canfield
  William, 102
Carlisle
  John, 73
Carr
  Joseph, 87
  William, 19, 20, 87, 97, 98
Carter
  Jeremiah, 107
  John, 22
  Robert, 29, 30, 31, 41, 78, 107, 109, 110
Chambers
  Thomas, 41
  William, 7
Chancellor
  Thomas, 90, 102
Chandler
  Elizabeth, 92
  Frances, 92, 93

Joseph, 92, 93
Mary, 92
Thomas, 92
Chilton
  John, 109, 110
  John S., 109, 110
  Thomas, 13, 36, 105
  Thomas, Jr., 20
Clark
  James, 10
  Robert, 11, 12
  Thomas, 95
Clayton
  Thomas, 14
Claytor
  Alvin, 22
  Anne, 22
  Elizabeth, 22
  John, 22
  Samuel, 22
  Thomas, 22
  William, 22
Cole
  Morris, 13, 14
Collins
  Christopher, 22
Connell
  Thomas, 87
Connelly
  Mary, 40, 74
  Patrick, 40
Conway
  Ann, 37, 38
Coombs
  John, 53, 76
Corbin
  Gawin, 17, 18, 93, 94
  Martha, 93, 94
  Richard, 93, 94, 107
Courtney
  James, 15, 24, 44, 47, 48, 104, 108
  Jeremiah, 24, 47, 48
  John, 44
  Leonard, 24

Westmoreland County, Virginia Deeds & Wills:
DB12, 1754-1756 and DB13, 1756-1761
Index

Margaret, 47, 48
Mary, 24
Samuel, 24, 104
Coward
  William, 44
Cox
  Eleanor, 108
  Elizabeth, 37, 38, 88
  Fleet, 23, 37, 38, 59
  George, 23
  Presley, 23
  Vincent, 11
  William, 109
Crabb
  Jane, 107
  John, 30, 31, 61, 62, 107
  Osmond, 31, 107
Crafford
  Peter, 50
Craig
  David, 28, 67
Craighill
  Elizabeth, 91
  William, 25, 81
Crange
  Samuel, 50
Crawford
  Thomas, 67, 68
Critcher
  Hester, 77
  John, 54
  Thomas, 77
Currie
  Alice, 84
  David, 84
  Jane, 84
Davis
  Anne, 24, 25
  Elias, 55
  Elizabeth, 59, 69, 70
  Gerrard, 37, 38
  Hugh, 15, 16, 59
  John, 69, 70
  Joshua, 24, 25

Peter, 59
Samuel, 24, 25
Thomas, 46, 69, 70
Thomas, Jr., 70
Degge
  James, 52, 72
  John, 5
  Mary, 13
  Tiperus, 13
  William, 5, 52, 72
Dishman
  James, 57, 58
  Mary, 53
  Samuel, 53
Douglass
  Robert, 94
Dowsitt
  John, 74
Dunbar
  William, 69, 73
Duncan
  Ann, 35
  William, 35
Dunkin
  Elizabeth, 50
  George, 50
  Sarah, 50
Durrant
  Thomas, 63
Earle
  Samuel, 39, 63
Edwards
  Anthony, 60
  Benjamin, 101, 102
  Jane, 101
  Meredith, 33
  William, 25
Eidsen
  Joseph, 32, 35, 99
Elliott
  Augustine, 25
  Elenor, 25
  Esther, 52
  John, 22, 25, 44, 45, 46

Westmoreland County, Virginia Deeds & Wills:
DB12, 1754-1756 and DB13, 1756-1761
Index

Robert, 25
William, 25
Elphinston
 James, 48
English
 Thomas, 24
Eskridge
 Abigail, 10
 Charles, 72, 73, 74
 George, 10, 11, 12, 31, 39, 72
 Hannah, 73, 74
 Robert, 10
 Samuel, 10, 72
 William, 103
Eustace
 Hancock, 84
Everett
 William, 35
Ewell
 Bertrand, 15
Farrell
 Francis, 15, 32
Faulkner
 Ralph, 79
Fauntleroy
 Henry, 70
Field
 Abraham, 97
 Henry, 20
Finch
 Ann, 53
 George, 53, 63
Fisher
 John, 10, 11, 64
Fleming
 John, 53, 54
Flood
 Frances, 86
 William, 86, 87
Footman
 John, 107
Frank
 Robert, 99
Franks,Henry, 29

Franks,Henry (Dr.), 29
Freek
 William, 79
French
 Hugh, 44
Fry
 Margaret, 56
Fuller
 Richard, 69
Garland
 William, 66, 83, 84, 100
Garner
 Abraham, 30, 31, 38, 39, 64, 65, 76, 107
 Bennett Abraham, 20
 Bradley, 44, 96
 Catherine, 65
 Henry, 96, 97
 James, 96
 Jeremiah, 69
 John, 23, 43, 44
 Joseph, 64, 65, 107
 Mary, 24, 96, 97
 Nathaniel, 65
 Parish, 108
 Rosamond, 24
 Thomas, 30
 Vincent, 30
Garrard
 Mary, 41
 William, 41, 42
Gilbert
 Francis, 100
 Michael, 54
 William, 26
Gill
 Lettice, 103
Gilpin
 William, 36
Goff
 Jane, 76
 Thomas O'Bryan, 76
 William O'Bryan, 76
Goffland

Westmoreland County, Virginia Deeds & Wills: DB12, 1754-1756 and DB13, 1756-1761
Index

William, 46
Graham
  John, 63
Gray
  Francis, 4, 5, 102
  George, 4, 5, 87, 88, 102
  Nathaniel, 4, 5, 102
Gregory
  James, 87
Grigsby
  Aaron, 101, 102
Haborn
  Eleanor, 54
Habron
  James, 15
Haikes
  Mary, 55, 56
  Richard, 55, 56, 65
Hall
  Ashton, 73, 76, 103, 104
  Leasure, 104
  Mary, 103, 104
  Presley, 104
  Richard Lingan, 94
Halliday
  Richard, 23, 30
Hardin
  Sarah, 89
  Thomas, 89
Hardwick
  Elizabeth, 74
  James, 74, 82
  Joseph, 41
  Thomas, 74
Harle
  Peter, 62
Harrison
  Alice, 26
  Daniel, 16, 53, 56
  Darkes, 16
  Frances, 88
  George, 16, 108
  Hannah, 28
  Jeremiah, 52, 56

  John, 54, 56
  John, Sr., 56
  Lovell, 28, 46, 47, 71
  Samuel, 6, 16, 31, 52, 54, 56
  William, 52
Hartley
  William, 6
Hawkins
  Richard, 9
Headley
  Robert, 108
Higdon
  John, 5, 6, 8, 27, 28, 42, 49
  Sarah, 49
Hilton
  Ann, 33
  John, 25, 32, 33, 67, 90, 91
Hipkins
  L., 87
Hopwood
  Richard, 63
Hore
  Elias, 68, 69
  James, 29
Howson
  Robert, 56
Hudson
  John, 65
  Joseph, 31
  Joshua, 56, 65
  Rush, 65
  Valentine, 65, 95, 96
Hughes
  Thomas, 45, 47, 92
Hunter
  John, 73, 74
Hurley
  John, 9
Hutcherson
  William, 50
Hutt
  Daniel, 89
  Gerard, 17, 59, 74, 89
  Gerard, Jr., 17, 74

Gerard, Sr., 17
Gerrard, 41, 74, 77
Gerrard, Jr., 41, 74
Mary, 41
Jackson
  Joseph, 36
  Nathan, 30
  Nathaniel, 40, 50
  Nathaniel, Jr., 50
  Richard, 14, 31, 36, 48, 61, 62, 98
  Sarah, 27
  William, 27
James
  Elizabeth, 12
  Thomas, 12
Jeffries
  Cisley, 10, 11, 12
  Edmund, 10, 11, 12
  George, 10, 11, 12, 66
  Jeremiah, 44
  Lettice, 10, 11, 12
Jerwood
  Thomas, 22
Jett
  Gladis, 78, 79
  John, 67, 79
  Peter, 79, 86, 99
Johnston
  Gabriel, 5, 19
  George, 95
Jolly
  Morris, 31
Jones
  Calvert, 90, 101
  David, 90, 101
Jordan
  John, 21, 22
Kendall
  William, 95
Kenner
  Brereton, 45, 46
King
  Samuel, 26
  Smith, 26

Lambeth
  Thomas, 58
Lamkin
  Ashton, 47, 108
  Daniel, 108
  George, 26
  Peter, 32, 35, 77, 99, 100, 108
Lane
  Elizabeth, 87
  James, 6, 52, 87, 102, 103
  Joseph, 6, 14, 15, 19, 20, 32, 37, 38, 87, 92, 93, 98, 103
  Martha, 103
  William, 19, 31, 41, 54, 102, 103
  William Carr, 103
  William, Sr., 19, 103
Lang
  Robert, 61
Lansdown
  John, 67
Lathrum
  John, 31
Lathukem
  Frankling, 20
Lawhon
  James, 97
Lawson
  Thomas, 40, 57, 96
Lee
  Francis Lightfoot, 20, 21, 94
  George, 60
  George, 40
  George, 61
  George, 96
  George (clerk), 5, 7, 8, 9, 10, 11, 12, 13, 14, 15, 16, 17, 18, 19, 20, 21, 22, 23, 24, 25, 27, 28, 29, 30, 31, 32, 33, 34, 35, 36, 37, 38, 39, 40, 41, 42, 43, 44, 47, 48, 49, 50, 51, 52, 53, 54, 55, 56, 57, 58, 59, 60, 61, 62, 63, 64, 65, 66, 67, 68, 69, 70, 71, 72, 73, 74, 76, 77, 78, 79, 80, 81, 82, 83, 84, 86, 87, 88, 89, 90, 91, 92, 93, 94, 96, 109, 110

Westmoreland County, Virginia Deeds & Wills:
DB12, 1754-1756 and DB13, 1756-1761
Index

   Henry, 14, 15, 16, 23, 32, 62, 94, 96, 97, 98
   Philip Ludwell, 40, 44, 62, 63
   Richard, 14, 15, 18, 19, 32, 36, 37, 38, 39, 40, 59, 60, 84, 92
   Richard Henry, 36, 93
   Thomas, 30, 93
   Thomas Ludwell, 29, 94
Lee, John, Jr. (deputy clerk), 94, 96, 97, 98, 99, 100, 101, 102, 103, 104, 105, 107
Lewis
   Vincent, 89
Love
   Samuel, 62, 63, 90
Lovell
   Jacob, 63
   John, 28, 50, 62, 63, 80
Lowe
   Richard, 10, 69
Luck
   Mary, 92, 94
Luttrell
   John, 51
Marmaduke
   William, 94
Martin
   Easter, 5
   John, 9, 23, 25, 28, 90, 91
   Mary Ann, 90
Mason
   James, 5, 8, 49
   John, 9, 27
Massey
   John, 95, 96
Mathias
   William, 87
McAuley
   Ann, 84
   Hannah, 7, 18
   Mary, 18
McCarty
   Daniel, 7, 13, 71
McCauley
   Charles, 50
McClan
   Paul, 44
McClane
   Catharine, 10
McFarlane
   Elizabeth, 37, 38
McKenny
   Daniel, 35, 103
   William, 41
Meakey
   Samuel, 90
Middleton
   Benedict, 6, 27
   Benjamin, 6, 26, 54, 77
   Elizabeth, 26
   Hannah, 103
   Jane, 26
   Jemima, 26
   Jeremiah, 26, 27, 54
   John, 59
   Robert, 27, 31, 59
   Robert, Jr., 27
   William, 26, 27, 54
Miller
   Elizabeth, 37, 38
Mills
   William, 52
Minor
   Nicholas, Jr., 20
Moberly
   Thomas, 89
Monday
   Robert, 101
Monroe
   Andrew, 28, 33, 50, 61
   Andrew, Jr., 53, 71
   Elizabeth, 53
   George, 85
   George, Jr., 34
   John, 28, 33, 53, 62, 63, 79, 80, 81, 87
   Rachael, 85
   Spence, 34, 42, 53, 71
   William, 21, 34, 65, 71, 85

Westmoreland County, Virginia Deeds & Wills: DB12, 1754-1756 and DB13, 1756-1761

Index

William, Sr., 34
Moon
  Robert, 77
Moore
  Richard, 69
  Robert, 58, 59
  Thomas, 54
  William, 11, 53, 54
Morgan
  John, 90
Morris
  Charles, 7
  Samuel, 89
  Thomas, 70
Morrison
  David, 70
Morton
  William, 25, 26, 51
Moss
  William, 34
Mothershead
  Alvin, 99
  Charles, 12
  Christopher, 90, 91
  Nathaniel, 22, 29
Moxley
  Daniel, 30, 31, 36
  Edward, 20, 21
  Elijah, 69
  Joseph, 36
  Richard, 20, 21, 35
  Samuel, 20
Mullins
  Elizabeth, 24
  John, 82
  Peter, 24, 47, 48
Munday
  Robert, 48
Murphy
  Elizabeth, 76
Muse
  Ann, 85, 88
  Edward, 29, 45
  John, 30, 45, 46, 47, 99

  Mary, 88
  Richard, 88
  Sarah, 88
  Thomas, 6, 25, 85, 88
Naughty
  James, 41, 42
  James, Jr., 41
  John, 30, 41, 42
Neale
  Christopher, 75
  Daniel, 30, 68, 75, 76
  Daniel, Jr., 67, 68
  John, 75
  Presley, 75
  Richard, 75
  Rodham, 75, 76
  Spence, 75, 76
Negroes
  Aaron, 91, 106
  Abigail, 106
  Abrabah, 106
  Abram, 106
  Adam, 106
  Alice, 106
  Andrew, 106
  Anthony, 106
  Bab, 106
  Baker, 106
  Bassett, 85
  Bazlzuv, 77
  Beck, 106
  Ben, 34, 77, 106
  Benn, 91
  Berry, 75
  Beth, 85
  Bett, 77
  Betty, 92, 106
  Betty's child Jenny, 92
  Billy, 106
  Bob, 21
  Boo, 106
  Boson, 75
  Bridget, 106
  Bristow, 77

Westmoreland County, Virginia Deeds & Wills: DB12, 1754-1756 and DB13, 1756-1761
Index

Cary, 86
Cate, 103, 106
Cesar, 106
Charity, 86, 106
Charlot, 106
Clark, 106
Conge, 75
Congo Tom, 88
Cuffy, 88
Cyrus, 94
Daniel, 106
Darkey, 105
Dawson, 106
Dick, 41, 48, 91, 103, 106
Dinah, 75, 106
Doz, 106
Easter, 106
Edy, 94
Emunidie, 48
Esaw, 106
Fortune, 77
Frank, 26, 85, 92, 106
George, 91, 92, 106
Grace, 106
Hannah, 12, 45, 77, 103, 106
Hany, 75
Harry, 59, 75, 85, 106
Harvey, 45, 106
Isaac, 86, 92, 106
Isaac (waiting man), 106
Jack, 77, 105, 106
Jacob, 88, 106
James, 75, 77, 85, 91
Jean, 75
Jem, 21
Jemima, 106
Jennis, 77
Jenny, 86, 88, 106
Jeny, 106
Jeto, 85
Joan, 88
Joan and her two children, 107
Joe, 91
John, 91

Joice, 106
Joseph, 86
Judah, 103
Jude and her young child, 91
Judea, 88
Judy, 85, 106
Keren, 105
Kezia, 106
Lett, 41
Lettice, 45, 91
Letty, 92
Little Tom, 88
Lucy, 75, 77, 106
Luke, 86
Magg, 103
Mamoth, 85
Mary, 54, 106
Milly, 85
Mimaur, 75
Mimy, 86
Moll, 12, 45, 88, 106
Mores, 106
Morly, 105
Mulatto Susanna, 54
Mullato Anne Potter, 58
Mullato Robin Wood, 55
Mullato William Potter, 58
Mullato Winifred Potter, 58
Nan, 75, 106
Nan, d/o Winey, 75
Nat, 106
Nate, 85
Ned, 106
Nell, 105
Nell & her son, 41
Nelll, 25
Nero, 106
Old Coffee, 91
Old Jenny, 88
Old Judah, 75
Old Sarah, 91
Pat, 106
Patience, 106
Patt, 86

Westmoreland County, Virginia Deeds & Wills: DB12, 1754-1756 and DB13, 1756-1761

Index

Peg, 106
Pegg, 26, 86
Peggy, 55
Pender, 85
Peter, 45, 58, 75, 86, 106
Philaday, 48
Phill, 106
Phillis, 105
Pompy, 85
Prew, 103
Ralph, 106
Rem, 85
Rhoda, 26
Rose, 45, 103
Sall, 77, 85
Sam, 86, 103, 106, 108
Sarah, 75, 85, 108
Scissis, 103
Sias, 85
Sibley, 75
Silly, 105
Simon, 106
Soloman, 106
Sukey, 106
Tim, 106
Toby, 103
Tom, 41, 75, 91, 92, 103, 106
Toney, 106
Tony, 26
Truelove, 94
Venus and her child, 48
Violet, 106
Wepster, 88
Whipster, 45
Will, 91, 92, 106
Willoughby, 106
Willy, 91
Winah, 106
Winey, 75
Winnie, 106
Winny, 77, 108
Young Coffee, 91
Young Sarah, 91
Newbury
  Robert, 103, 104
Newgent
  Robert, 64
Newton
  John, 6, 13, 14, 36, 43, 54, 66, 97, 98
  Willoughby, 36, 48, 54, 56, 57, 61, 96, 97, 98
Nicholson
  Mary, 70
Norwood
  John, 39
Oldham
  Samuel, 18, 48, 66
Omohundro
  John, 40, 41
  John, Jr., 40, 41
  William, 41
Palmer
  Thomas, 78
Parker
  Richard, 55, 87
Parkington
  Mary, 35, 36
Partridge
  Jane, 108
  Matthew, 72, 107, 108
Peach
  Thomas, 90
Pearce
  Richard, 46
Peirce
  Joseph, 87
  Sarah Elliott, 55
Pendleton
  Nathaniel, 51
Perry
  Franklin, 88
  Susannah, 88
Pettit
  John, 70, 106
  Lydia Bushrod, 106
Peyton
  Anthony, 92
  John, 92

Westmoreland County, Virginia Deeds & Wills: DB12, 1754-1756 and DB13, 1756-1761

Index

Pierce
  William, 68
Piper
  Ann, 85
  Benjamin, 85, 86
  David, 85
  John, 67, 85, 86
  Jonathan, 85
  Mary, 85, 86
  William, 85, 86, 99
Places
  Aberdeen (North Britain), 48
  Bluff Point, 63
  Bradley's Point, 65
  Brereton Neck, 44, 45, 46
  Broad Neck, 22
  Courtney's Mill, 47
  Covent Garden, London, 29
  Double Mill, 19, 87
  Haw Point, 65
  Hollowing Poynt Neck, 97
  Hudson's Landing, 55
  Jett's Mill, 79
  Long's Warehouse (London), 29
  Machodoc Neck, 19, 44, 60
  Muster Field, 51
  Narrows Point, 97
  Nominy Warehouse, 105
  Norwich (England), 29
  Pope's Quarter, 48
  Potomac River, 66, 76
  Ragged Point Neck, 38, 64, 76
  Richmond Church Yard, 29
  Round about Hill, 24
  Round Hill Church, 5, 102
  Rust's Mill, 44
  Rust's Warehouses, 17
  Scutt's Point, 65
  Simpson's Quarter, 77
  Storke's Dam, 33
  Washington's Mill, 79, 102
  Weedon's Dam, 9, 90
  Yeocomico Church, 39, 57
  Yeocomico Neck, 10, 13, 39, 61, 62

Pope
  Benjamin, 99
  Charles, 71
  Humphrey, 6, 30, 99
  John, 99
  Mary, 71, 99
  Nathaniel, 71, 72, 99
  Sarah, 99
  Thomas, 71
Porter
  William, 51
Potes
  William, 95
Price
  Evan, 20
  Grace, 20
  Jane, 91
  John, 20, 25
  Mary, 20
  Sarah, 20
  Thomas, 89, 90
  William, 42
Pritchett
  Amy, 21
  Rodham, 14, 23
Proctor
  Isaac, 26
Purland
  Matthew, 28, 29
Quisenberry
  Christopher, 22
  William, 16, 17, 31, 32, 34, 35
  William, Sr., 16, 17, 31, 34
Rallings
  Margaret, 78, 79, 80
  Samuel, 78, 79, 80
Randall
  Francis, 94
  Samuel, 71
Rankins
  Hopkins, 63
Ransdell
  Edward, 44, 46, 54, 55, 76, 109, 110
  Elizabeth, 76

Westmoreland County, Virginia Deeds & Wills: DB12, 1754-1756 and DB13, 1756-1761
Index

Sarah, 55
Wharton, 13, 54, 55
William, 55
Read
  Andrew, 89
  Coleman, 35, 89
  Ruth, 89
Redman
  John, 109, 110
  Joseph, 74
  Stewart, 40
Rice
  Isabella, 58
  John, 58
  Mary, 58
  Simon, 58
  Zorabable, 58
Roberts
  Elizabeth, 104
Robinson
  Anne, 17
  Frances, 51
  James, 17, 41, 74
  John, 17
  Maximilian, 70
  Michael, 51, 52
  Richard, 17
  Thomas, 17, 41, 82
  Thomas Redman, 17, 41
  William, 17, 41
Rochester
  John, 77
  Mary, 63, 64
  William, 63, 64, 98
Roe
  Bunch, 21, 71
  Henry, 21, 53, 70, 71
  William, 21
Rowe
  William, 33
Rowzee
  John, 25
Rozier
  David, Jr., 98

Russell
  James, 45
  James, Sr., 46
Rust
  Ann, 109
  Benjamin, 30
  George, 11, 27, 104
  Jeremiah, 52
  John, 108, 109
  Peter, 10, 63, 64, 66, 73
  Samuel, 24, 43, 44, 108
  Sarah, 108
  Vincent, 17, 99, 100
Sanders
  Philip, 40
  William, 40
Sandy
  Vincent, 7
Sanford
  Augustine, 12, 13, 51, 52, 88, 89, 94
  Dorcas, 51
  Edward, 30, 88
  James, 104, 105
  John, 12, 13, 31, 89, 105
  Katherine, 89
  Margaret, 51
  Richard, 21, 51, 88, 89
  Robert, 13, 35, 36, 88, 104, 105
  Robert, Sr., 13
  Susannah, 88
  Thomas, 35, 36, 51, 52, 55
  William, 36
  Willoughby, 35, 36
  Winifred, 105
  Youell, 51
Self
  Catherine, 57
  Francis, 57
  Stephen, 14, 47
  Thomas, 23
  William, 23
Settle
  Elizabeth, 65
  Francis, 9, 87, 88, 90, 102

Westmoreland County, Virginia Deeds & Wills:
DB12, 1754-1756 and DB13, 1756-1761
Index

Margaret, 55, 56
Sarah, 9, 87, 88, 90, 102
Shadrach
   Thomas, 45
Shaw
   John, 49
   Thomas, 46, 70, 71
Short
   John, 16
Simpson
   Joseph, 35
   Thomas, 18
Sims
   Job, 42, 43
Slaughter
   Thomas, 51
Smith
   Abraham, 97
   Augustine, 25
   Eleanor, 58, 59
   James, 77, 78
   John, 29
   Mary, 77, 78
   Peter, 58, 59
   Samuel, 54, 59, 96
   Stephen, 59
   Susanna, 82
   William, 79, 82, 100
Sorrell
   John, 36, 37, 38
   Judith, 36, 37, 38
South
   Jemima, 105
Spark
   Alexander, 48, 69, 70
Speke
   Thomas, 9
Spence
   John, 68, 78
   Patrick, 94
   Thomas, 21, 31
Spencer
   John, 7
   Nicholas, 39

Spiller
   Dorothy, 95
Spillman
   John, 86, 99
   Margaret, 98
   Thomas, 99
   William, 86, 98, 99
Stapleton
   Elizabeth, 15, 16
   Thomas, 15, 16
Steele
   Richard, 47, 70
Stephens
   Burditt, 63
Steptoe
   Ann, 39, 40
   Elizabeth, 39, 40, 61, 62, 66, 84
   George, 39, 40
   James, 18, 39, 40, 61, 62, 66, 72
   Thomas, 39, 40
Stone
   Joseph, 51
Storke
   John, 8, 23, 33, 46
Stowers
   John, 39
Strother
   John, 5
   Sarah, 5, 57, 58
Sturman
   Foxhall, 51
   John, 9, 51, 97
Suggett
   James, 25, 26, 51
   Jemima, 51
Taylor
   James, 85
   Thomas, 27, 33, 34, 50, 58, 61
   William, 41, 70
   William Woods, 29
Tebbs
   Daniel, 6, 11, 12, 14, 15, 19, 26, 31,
      37, 38, 39, 47, 48, 61, 62, 66, 72, 73,
      74

Daniel, Jr., 18, 47, 48, 73
Mary, 36, 37, 38
William, 14, 15, 36, 37, 38
Templeman
  William, 48, 49
Thomas
  Elizabeth, 87
  William, 87
Thompson
  Andrew, 95
  James, 79, 80
Thornbury
  John, 101
  Samuel, 101
Thornton
  Anthony, 95
Tidwell
  John, 32, 77, 78
  Robert, 19, 20
  William Carr, 19, 20, 97, 98
Triplett
  James, 68, 69
  John, 9, 68, 69, 79, 85, 90
  William, 68, 69
Trussell
  Matthew, 57
Turberville
  George, 98
  John, 86, 87, 97, 98
  Martha, 97, 98
Tyler
  William, 21
Underwood
  Mary, 49
Vaulx
  Betty, 44, 45
  Caty, 44, 45, 47
  Elizabeth, 46
  Kenner, 44
  Milly, 44, 46
  Molly, 44, 46
  Robert, 44, 47, 69, 70
  Sally, 44
  Sarah, 46

Vickers
  John (Vicars), 68, 69
Vigour
  William, 46
Walker
  Elizabeth, 103
  Felicity, 19
  John, 83, 84
  Richard, 83, 84
  William, 19, 44, 63, 103
  William, Jr., 63
Washington
  Ann, 42, 43, 46
  Augustine, 44, 45, 46, 47
  Hannah, 105, 106
  Henry, 42, 43
  Jeanny, 105
  John, 36, 42, 43
  John Augustine, 107
  Lawrence, 33, 45
  Mary, 105
  Thomas, 36
Watercourse
  Aquia Creek, 55
  Attopin Creek, 24
  Beaver Dam Run, 55
  Bonham's Creek, 13
  Clayton's Run, 13
  Cool Springs Branch, 84
  Crabb's Creek, 37, 38
  Double Mill Pond, 74, 87
  Flints Mill Creek, 17, 84
  Gammer Masseys Spring, 5
  Horse Swamp, 45
  Hudson's Cove, 55
  Hurd's Creek, 30, 31, 76
  Jackson's Creek, 76
  Kings Creek, 9, 73
  Lower Machodoc River, 97
  Machodoc Creek, 55
  Mattox Creek, 8, 27, 28, 49, 60, 79, 81
  Miry Branch, 22
  Negro Run (Culpeper County), 108
  Nominy Creek, 8, 9

Westmoreland County, Virginia Deeds & Wills: DB12, 1754-1756 and DB13, 1756-1761
Index

Nominy River, 109, 110
Peter Lamkin's Mill Pond, 108
Pohick Run, 39
Potomack River, 31, 38
Rotank Creek, 13
Roziers Creek, 42, 43, 90
Rust's Mill Pond, 63
Tanyard Swamp, 108
Tebbs Run, 47
Tuckers Run, 57
Upper Machodoc Creek, 50
Vincent Rust's Spring Branch, 17
Vinyard Branch, 37, 38
Ward's Creek, 73
Wolf Pit Swamp, 40
Yeocomico Creek, 17
Yeocomico River, 17, 83, 100

Watts
  George, 97
  William, 97
Weaver
  Sarah, 105
  William, 32
Webb
  Elias, 68
Weedon
  George, 57
  John, 21, 24, 96
Weeks
  Benjamin, 29, 31, 47, 54
Welch
  John, 56
West
  John, 31
Wheeler
  Ann, 89, 90
  William, 89, 90
White
  George, 35
  John, 78
  Richard, 82
Whitfield
  James, 51, 52, 60

Whiting
  Lizey, 53
  Molly, 53
  Nelly, 53
  Thomas, 21, 53
Wiggington
  Henry, 14, 37, 38
Wilkinson
  Elizabeth, 104
  Garard, 104
  James, 60, 61
  James, 104
  John, 60, 104
  Mary, 60
  Robert, 104
  Thomas, 104
  Tyler, 104
  William, 104
Williams
  Francis, 25, 46, 47, 82, 92
  John, 57, 59
  Margaret, 91
  Thomas, 31, 82
  William, 51
Winslow
  Thomas, 39
Winter
  Daniel, 77
Woodson
  James, 14, 15, 32
Wright
  Francis, 53, 108, 109
  Thomas, 12, 74
Wroe
  Elizabeth, 71, 72
  Original, 25, 58, 61, 65, 79
  William, 24, 25, 71, 72
Yeates
  Traverse, 32
Youell
  Thomas, 97

Made in the USA
Columbia, SC
03 April 2023